THE
LOWBROW
READER
READER

Edited by Jay Ruttenberg

✖✖✖ Drag City | Chicago

CONTENTS

Harpo Marx illustration by *Nathan Gelgud*

Illustrations by *David Berman, Carl Cassel, Carson Ellis, Nathan Gelgud,
Jackie Gendel, Doreen Kirchner, M. Sweeney Lawless, John Mathias,
Alex Eben Meyer, Phillip Niemeyer, Mike Reddy and Tom Sanford*

INTRODUCTION

I N THE FALL of 2000, with no small amount of trepidation, I
moved to New York City, prospects low and dreams high. I
was 24. While relocating to the city rarely comes without hic-
cups, for me it proved thoroughly traumatic. I'm sure my ances-
tors, upon arriving penniless at Ellis Island, experienced some
degree of hardship—but then, they were not attempting to land
a job in media and a rent-stabilized one-bedroom downtown.

Although I lack the documentation to prove anything con-
clusively, it is my suspicion that prior to my arrival, the populace
of lower Manhattan had gathered to plot various ways to thwart
me. Thus, a job slipped through my fingers, as did approximately
14,297 apartments leads. My girlfriend, shockingly, began to
grow annoyed at my unremitting stream of kvetching. Friends
suggested that I consider a living situation more suited to my
temperament, such as my parents' basement back in suburban
Chicago. Nothing was clicking.

But as New York pummels its newcomers, it simultaneously
seduces them. Within days, I had fallen into the grip of this
town that was laboring so intensely to cut me down. If I were to
stay, it struck me as vulgar not to contribute something, however slight, to the city's cultural ecosystem. As I skulked about
the streets, my eyes glued to the pavement and my shoulders
hunched in defeat, I formed an odd yet somehow unquenchable

desire to launch a small comedy journal. In the past, such an idea would have been banished to the recesses of my mind. Invigorated by my new urban life, as if possessed by the holy spirit of Alfred E. Neuman himself, I began plotting and scheming.

My thought was to combine original humor pieces with writing about comedy—specifically, the "lowbrow" comedy at which critics so often scoffed. It galled me that a movie like *Billy Madison*, which I considered a masterpiece, had been so reviled by newspaper reviewers. And there seemed a general dearth of writing about comedy, especially when compared with the fawning reporting on other corners of entertainment—most egregiously mainstream indie-rock, which even then was covered to a degree bordering on the absurd. In the *Lowbrow Reader*, I wanted to raise a tiny voice of opposition.

Shunning telephone and e-mail, I hopped a Greyhound bus to Boston to meet my friend Matt Berube, who had just wrapped publication on his literary journal, the *Swim*. Berube had long struck me as being at once multitalented and ferociously honorable—the type of New Englander to whom mayors should entrust their keys and farmers their daughters. We went to Dunkin' Donuts. Emboldened by my new Manhattan energy, I peppered Matt with my plans and asked if he would be interested in designing the zine. I suspect I hung around Boston for at least another day, but in memory, I boarded a bus back to New York the moment he enlisted.

Returned to the city, I attempted to fathom what this comedy journal would encompass. I envisioned a large group of writers and comedians contributing outlandish comic reporting. But I hardly knew anybody of this ilk, so instead gave fake names to some pieces I had written in order to create the illusion of a collective. I added some other features—an essay about Howard Stern's recent divorce, a funny Three Stooges spoof by a comedian friend, a mock editorial praising Will Ferrell's impression of the inept Texas governor George Bush—but I was more or less stumped.

In time, I found a job writing about music for *Time Out New York*—a two-week temp gig that, to my salvation and distress, ultimately would endure for more than a decade. Very early in my tenure there, I interviewed the musician and writer Neil Hagerty. I had met Hagerty in the past with his old band, Royal Trux, first interviewing him for my college newspaper and later traveling to his house in the Virginia countryside to write an article for my beloved previous employer, *Puncture* magazine. I was a tremendous admirer of Hagerty's work; perhaps because I had first encountered him when I was an impressionable teen, he struck me as some kind of rogue oracle.

STERN RULES FOR STERN TIMES
by Jay Ruttenberg
Illustration by Francesca Granata

There's one word behind the collapse of Howard Stern's 21-year marriage–obsession. The super-popular radio shock jock became so obsessed with his work that he no longer had time to spend with his wife Alison and their three daughters, a source close to Howard revealed. ... 'This is a terribly painful time for Howard, even though he's not wearing his heart on his sleeve. He knows the reality is that he chose his career over his family.'
THE NATIONAL ENQUIRER

It would be an insult to the disc jockey's true devotees if I called myself a Howard Stern fan. For the last five years or so my alarm clock has been set for 11:11 a.m., which means that, with rare exception, by the time I open my ears in the morning his radio show has ended. When I do happen to catch the Stern show—when the sun somehow outmaneuvers my window shade, when I have to pick somebody up at the airport, when I consume too much cereal milk the previous night—I vow to shift my sleeping schedule so I can listen more frequently. But I never manage to do this, and so I never listen to Howard Stern.

I have, however, followed the deejay closely enough to understand the magnitude of his marital separation. Assuming that it is not an extremely intense publicity stunt (he wouldn't dare!), this is, by a long shot, the most "shocking" act of his public life.

Contrary to popular opinion, Howard Stern does not represent any of the following:

lowest common denominator potty humor
degradation of American society
complete breakdown of FCC regulations
national obsession with cheap (and often lesbian) eroticism
criminally bad hair

Rather, Stern is the disgusted clown with a motor-mouth of sewage and a heart of sugar. His brains aren't where he sits but where he applies Carmex,

20 THE LOWBROW READER

SUMMER 2001 21

Stern Rules for Stern Times / Lowbrow Reader #1

During our interview in Manhattan, we got to talking about Redd Foxx—how could we not?!—and I told Neil about the comedy zine I was struggling to cook up. "You should write for it!" I blurted out. I thought little of this exchange until a few weeks later, when he e-mailed me with ideas for three articles: two about recent movies and a third about the eccentric, long-shuttered auto-humor magazine *CARtoons*. "The first two pitches sound great," I wrote back. "But I don't know anything about *CARtoons*, so maybe not the third."

"In that case," Hagerty replied, "I will write the third idea, *CARtoons*."

And so it went. Before long, I was put in touch with an illustrator, John Mathias, who agreed to draw a cartoon portraying a Japanese fop taking his daily. His illustration was so chic that Berube and I put it on the cover; as the years ticked on, we decided to devote every *Lowbrow* cover to a Mathias toilet gag.

By the summer of 2001, I triumphantly boarded a bus to Boston once more so that Matt and I could put the finishing

Contents, Quartet for Three Strings and a Talking Jew / Lowbrow Reader #1

touches on *Lowbrow Reader* #1. The issue was spotty and grasping for a voice. Yet Berube's design was elegant and tidy, the *CARtoons* article popped, and the cover was superior to anything I had imagined producing. As it turned out, Berube, Hagerty and Mathias understood what I wanted to do better than I did myself.

Over the next decade, the *Lowbrow* rolled along at a leisurely pace and, in my not-at-all biased opinion, grew stronger and stronger. Of course, this self-proclaimed (and, I should add, still unrecognized) success came through no fault of my own: With each issue, the journal broadened its ranks to a smart pool of writers and artists. This circle would extend to close friends and strangers whose work I long admired; family members and co-workers; gifted neighbors from Chelsea and inspired nutters in far-flung time zones. It would include vibrant drawings by Mike Reddy, Tom Sanford, Doreen Kirchner and the other wholly distinct artists represented in these pages, while incorporating the wild interviews of Margeaux Rawson, literary excavation of Jay Jennings, deadline poems of M. Sweeney Lawless, inimitable musings of Gilbert Rogin, and scribbling by other heroes of the table-of-contents page. Their work has made the *Lowbrow Reader* much better than it should have been. I hope this anthology does justice to their toil while capturing the spirit of the journal; I hope the *Lowbrow Reader* has added some worthy, microscopic crumb to New York's cultural ecosystem.

....

A few years after we began publication, I was visiting my parents in Chicago and my father was helping me with my taxes. That is to say, my father was doing my taxes as I sat next to him sullen and witless, like a dim, overgrown teenager. "Now what about this year's *Lowbrow Reader* expenses?" he inquired.

I jerked to life, beaming with pride to report my news. "This year," I imperiously announced, "we broke even."

My dad turned away from his computer and eyed me pityingly. "Do you have a plan for this thing?" he asked. "When do you hope to start making money on it?"

"Oh, that's not really the point," I cheerfully replied.

My father removed his glasses and leaned back in his chair. He stared at his futile eldest son and, though momentarily silent, palpably appeared on the brink of epiphany. "I think I get the *Lowbrow Reader*," he said at last. "It's an ego thing."

Jay Ruttenberg
Foggia, Italy
2011

COVER GALLERY

Illustrations by John Mathias
Design by Matthew Berube

THE

LOWBROW READER

of Basement Brow Comedy

ISSUE 1 ... SUMMER 2001 ... $2.50

Lowbrow Reader #1, 2001

THE

LOWBROW READER

of Basement Brow Comedy

ISSUE 2 ... SUMMER 2002 ... $3.00

Lowbrow Reader #2, 2002

The
LOWBROW READER
of Basement Brow Comedy

INSIDE
Queens of Comedy,
Yiddish Curses,
Lou Reed, Sandler,
Stern, more...

ISSUE 3
SUMMER 2003
US $3.00

Lowbrow Reader #3, 2003

The

LOWBROW READER

of Basement Brow Comedy

INSIDE
*Wings, Larry David,
Ol' Dirty Bastard,
Jackie Mason, more...*

ISSUE 4
FALL 2004
US $3.00

JNM
'04

Lowbrow Reader #4, 2004

THE RETURN OF THE BEAR
by John Mathias

The

LOWBROW READER

of Lowbrow Comedy

ISSUE 5
SUMMER 2006
US $3.00

INSIDE
The White Stripes, Joan Rivers,
Don Knotts, Chevy Chase, more...

www.lowbrowreader.com

Lowbrow Reader #5, 2006

The

LOWBROW READER
of Lowbrow Comedy

INSIDE
Gene Wilder, Class Warfare,
Overlooked Comedies, more...

lowbrowreader.com

ISSUE 6
US $3.00

Lowbrow Reader #6, 2008

The

LOWBROW READER
of Lowbrow Comedy

INSIDE
Gilbert Rogin, Shelley Berman,
Don Rickles, more...

lowbrowreader.com

ISSUE 7
US $3.00

Lowbrow Reader #7, 2009

The

LOWBROW READER
of Lowbrow Comedy

INSIDE
Clowns, Cartoons, Billy Madison,
Muhammad Ali, more...

lowbrowreader.com

ISSUE 8
US $3.00

Lowbrow Reader #8, 2010

WHEN RICKLES SINGS

by Jay Ruttenberg

D ON RICKLES FANS—what a sour lot! Front-row masochists and back-of-the-room cowards, Rat Pack fetishists and young men intrigued with old Vegas, nasty uncreative types prowling for put-downs and men's magazine subscribers with a misplaced sense of the ironic.

And yet Don Rickles himself—what a guy! He's curmudgeonly and cute, a wrinkly Yoda with an attitude problem. Deep into his 80s, he remains one of the world's quickest talk-show guests. (Chris Rock, the reigning champion of the couch, credits Rickles with drawing his blueprint.) He is world famous as an "insult comic" and yet is a notoriously kindhearted soul. He's an improbable unifier: the man who allegedly doesn't like anybody, liked by everybody.

Last fall, Rickles headlined three nights at New York's Town Hall. This was the same stage show captured in John Landis's documentary *Mr. Warmth: The Don Rickles Project*, but somehow it seemed far stranger in person. The show is embalmed in time. A bald singer opens with a Frank Sinatra tribute. "I'm just a guy from Brooklyn," he says, "and here I am, at Town Hall." Rickles wears a tux, putters about the stage like a Florida retiree searching for his keys. In an age of solitary comics, he performs in front of an orchestra. Toward the end of the show, he introduces the VIPs scattered around the audience—Paul Shaffer!

Cedric the Entertainer! Regis!—and insults them. He cracks jokes informed by Greatest Generation stereotypes, slanty-eyed Orientals and the like, but he holds no bile. When I saw Jackie Mason a few months earlier, his bigotry seemed genuine and ugly, as if his every summer weekend had been ruined by the stupidity of Polacks and sloth of schvartzes; Rickles delivers his slurs so lovingly, they seem like compliments. When he dies, the comic will be halted at the gates of heaven by awed gods, eagerly awaiting their insults.

A few years ago, I briefly spoke with Rickles by phone. (He was giving me a quote about another comedian, who I was profiling for a magazine.) Rickles greeted me with a gentle, somewhat obligatory insult; then the rancor melted away, revealing a warm and soft-spoken old man. His act follows a similar pattern. He frontloads the insults, his calling card. Even given his repute, the comic can seem shockingly cruel—but what are people thinking being overweight, or of German descent, or comely, or old, and attending a Don Rickles performance? As the show

Catholics **Polacks** The Two-Four Club Dean Folks, we're all brothers. Frank
moron The Sands **Japs** Frankie saved my life once. He said, "That's enough, boys." Stupid Pat McCormick **Wop**
hockey puck **Sammy** Hooker Queers
idiot my mother How much do you weigh, Tiny? **Mob** Vegas black
guy with a radio **Mafia** When the ship goes down we'll see if those are real. Marty Scorsese Irish
drunk the Pope Atlantic City sweetheart **Bob Newhart** Mexicans
Give me a hug. Did any rub off? prostitute **Jew** Tropicana **brassiere** Wetback Polack
bimbo **Casino** dummy Johnny Carson Who picked your tie, Helen Keller?

Text cloud by M. Sweeney Lawless

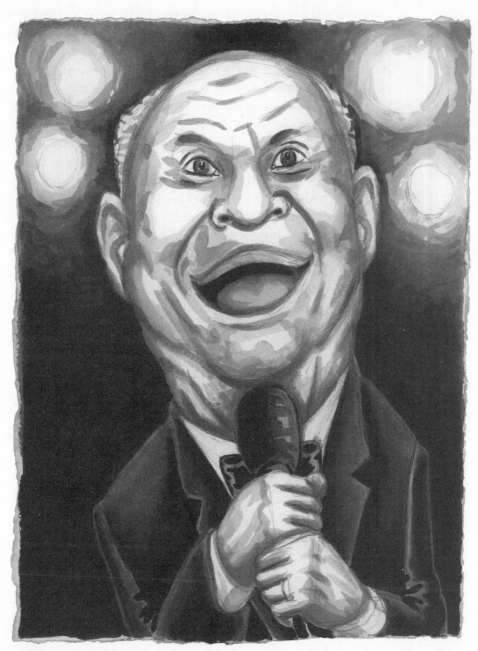

Illustration by Tom Sanford

wears on and his glass empties, the comedian turns increasingly to the maudlin. Night after night, tears well in his eyes as he salutes his late mother (he is a notorious mama's boy); he gives a hokey spiel about the worth of friends and toasts Sinatra, under whose spell he remains. And then, in the night's most berserk portion, Rickles fires up the orchestra and sings.

Only a lunatic would attend a Don Rickles show for the music. Nonetheless, night after night, the comic weaves in and out of these songs that nobody wants to hear. Like many stand-ups, he sings with natural flow and big personality, his voice trembling and sweet. Next to Rickles, Joan Baez seems insincere and Thom Yorke lighthearted. Yet his music's earnestness is no more a front than his comedy's wrath: Rickles was molded in an age that predated the cultural saturation of unblinking irony. It is difficult to imagine callous-minded comedians of subsequent generations breaking into heartfelt song. At the same time, none of these heirs are as merciless as their savage elder. Herein lies the magic of Rickles's songs: They are windows to his vulnerability and thus his license to kill. They reinforce the true punch line to the comedian's "Mr. Warmth" moniker—its veracity—while granting this nice old man permission to unleash his ferocious hoard of million-dollar insults.

Lowbrow Reader #7, 2009

THE QUEENS OF COMEDY ON THE COMMANDMENTS OF SEX

by Margeaux Rawson

IN 2001, *Glamour* magazine assigned entertainment jour-nalist Margeaux Rawson to interview the four Queens of Comedy—Adele Givens, Miss Laura Hayes, Mo'Nique and Sommore—about sex. The specific assignment was to uncover the "10 Commandments of Sex," as decried by the Queens. Armed with all the buffalo wings and bottles of Veuve Clicquot her expense account could manage, the writer met the quartet of comediennes in a Los Angeles hotel suite. Alas, it appears as if the champagne and chicken should have been left in New York: *Glamour* deemed every inch of the transcript too "blue" for its perfume-scented pages. *Lowbrow*, on the other hand, con-sidered the interview just lewd enough....

LOWBROW READER: As you all probably know, today's assignment is to come up with the 10 Commandments of sex.

SOMMORE: Rule number one is see his ID and make sure he is who he say he is. Rule number two: Wash that ass! Wash that ass! Wash that ass!

MO'NIQUE: That's rules three, four, five and six! Another rule: Must eat pussy! I know you can't print that, but that's rule number 10 through 59. Must be a pussy-licker. Ain't no pussy-licker, you gotta get away from me.

SOMMORE: I ain't really into that. I'm selective about who I let eat my pussy because everybody don't take care of their teeth.

ADELE: Sommore, if it was a fight between pussy and teeth, pussy gon' tear them teeth up every time. Don't worry about it, cause that pussy gon' tear them teeth up!

SOMMORE: Hmm-mmm. I ain't wit' it.

ADELE: Oral sex is an art. It's kinda like rap and comedy: Everybody think they can do it but they can't. And if the right person do it to you, you ain't gonna never have it no other way. You gon' be like, "You got to go [*singing*] downtown!" When it's right, it's like crack.

SOMMORE: Let me tell you something, a nigga will bust a goddamn root canal trying to make me come.

ADELE: That's cause he ain't shit!

SOMMORE: No, that's cause I use vibrators.

LAURA: That's another commandment! Don't be scared of my toys.

SOMMORE: Involve food. I had somebody put some whipped cream on me. Honey is nice, too.

ADELE: Well, I ain't got time for food. We eat *before*—we might go to dinner or something.

MO'NIQUE: Nah, bitch! That's not what she means. She means

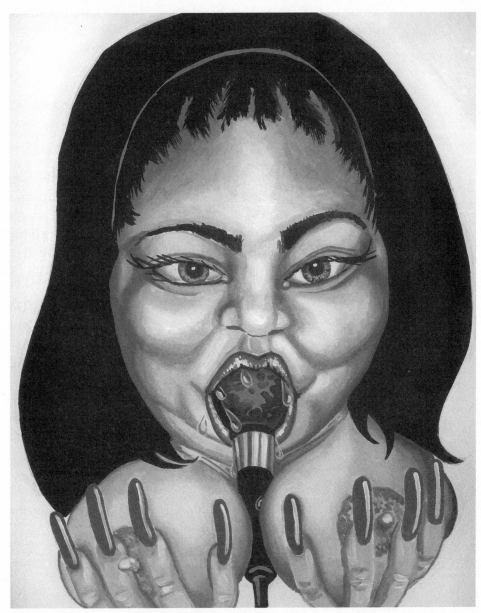

Mo'Nique / Illustration by Tom Sanford

taking a strawberry and inserting it till the pointy piece is sticking out. Then you see his skills—if he can suck the whole strawberry.

ADELE: What?!

MO'NIQUE: Let a muthafucka eat a strawberry out your pooty-cat!

SOMMORE: Noise is a must. You gotta make some noise.

MO'NIQUE: Yes! And you gotta talk the nastiest, filthiest shit you can imagine. Call me a bitch! Call me all kinds of bitches and hoes and sluts. Oooh! I like that! Call me a dirty bitch, nasty bitch, stanky bitch.... And you gotta be a little rough. Hit a bitch in the back of her head. *Pow!* Smack my hair up. Kick a bitch in her back. *Bam!*

SOMMORE: Grab a bitch's ass and spread her cheeks open. Do something surprising.

MO'NIQUE: Bitch! You better watch yourself! Now, I have a thing with walls. You *must* be able to fuck on a wall.

LAURA: That's why I like a hallway—the wall in front of you is for you to balance on, but he's behind you with his back against the other wall. You got all the power.

MO'NIQUE: Can I say one thing? The ear means nothing! Don't lick the ear. It don't tingle. It don't do shit. It's like licking the kneecap. What the fuck are you doing that for?

LAURA: The behind is cool.

MO'NIQUE: Have you tried Altoids yet?

LAURA: Uh-uh.

MO'NIQUE: Put an Altoid in his mouth and let him suck it till it gets real small. Then let him eat your pussy. Baby, it's a sensation!

ADELE: Toothpaste, peppermint—all of 'em do the same thing.

MO'NIQUE: But Altoids is the best by far.

SOMMORE: You gotta be able to dance sexy. And sucking dick ain't never killed nobody.

ADELE: Keep your shoes on when you dancing. Sometimes, keep your shoes on the whole time.

SOMMORE: And suck your own titties. Niggas like that.

MO'NIQUE: You ever been fucked so hard it bring your period on when you was supposed to come three days later? You fucked so hard and then you look and you like, "Oh, damn! I'm bleeding. Shit!"

FOUR QUEENS IN UNISON: Yes!

MO'NIQUE: You ever been fucked so hard you don't remember falling asleep? You don't even remember that nigga pulling out?

ADELE: I like to be raped like that. I used to get raped like that all the time, cause I can't hold liquor. Tony [Adele's husband] used to give me champagne and I used to wake up butt naked. He had a thrill doing that. I'd say, "You'se a fucking freak!" I'd wake up and his DNA is all over me. I'm like, "What the fuck happened?" And he's like [in a sweet voice], "I don't know." Well, ain't nobody here but me and you, nigga!

LAURA: [*mockingly*] Whose DNA is this?

ADELE: He'd be passing me drinks. If you ever notice when me and Tony go out and I start drinking, he gives me all that liquor. He know what he gonna be doing. He do whatever the fuck he want to me, and I like it. When I wake up I don't even know what you did, muthafucka, but it's everywhere. You had a ball with my dead ass. I was laying there asleep.

SOMMORE: I swallowed one time and I had gas for the longest. But you know what? Men like when you pretend to swallow. Just let it go in your mouth and run out the side of your mouth.

LAURA: It reminds me of castor oil. I've done tried it. I did my best. [*Adele starts singing a negro spiritual.*] But it just won't happen, and the only thing I can associate it with is when I had to take castor oil when I was little. I can't get rid of it. I'm 51. I'm probably not gonna get rid of it. So don't fuck with me like that.

MO'NIQUE: I can tell if my man's been drinking in his come. I can tell what he's been eating. It has such a bitter taste to it and it stays with you forever.

SOMMORE: Be tight on your dick-sucking skills. See, I love sucking dick. I think it's the bomb. I love it! I would rather suck somebody's dick than fuck them.

ADELE: You *gotta* love it. I got passion when I'm sucking your dick. This is the Popsicle, goddamit, that a bitch got when the ice-cream man came. You gotta have the same passion. It's a commandment to women. Or hell, sissies.

LOWBROW READER: Have you ever had sex with someone whose come had a strange consistency?

ADELE: The muthafucka probably got prostate cancer and he don't even know it. You be like, "You know what, dude? You need to go see your doctor. You ain't even got no salt in your shit. Something's wrong."

MO'NIQUE: Or they got brown come. You be like, What the fuck?

LOWBROW READER: How about role playing?

MO'NIQUE: I like that. Mine is a little insurance agent. He put his little suit on and carries a briefcase.

SOMMORE: My imagination ain't that good.

MO'NIQUE: You into just straight fucking.

SOMMORE: I like the dick. Really, that's just it. I can come from sucking a dick. And this is another thing too: I can take you eating my pussy if you nasty. But if you just a regular ol' church boy and you decide today that you gonna eat some pussy.... You gotta be a real nasty muthafucka and eat the pussy, if you gonna eat the pussy. And don't play with my ass, either. I'll tell you right now, if you lick my ass, I'm gonna look at you different tomorrow. I'll look at your mama different.

ADELE: Right! I ain't gonna drop you now. But, nigga, tomorrow I'm gonna ignore you.

SOMMORE: Nigga, if you lick my ass, guess what? I'm looking at you different.

MO'NIQUE: No! Ass-licking is a commandment!

LOWBROW READER: You *want* ass-licking?

MO'NIQUE: You muthafuckin' right. Ass-licking is a commandment. You better lick my ass! And then, if you lick it well enough, I might let you put the head in. Lick my ass! That is a wonderful thing. Lick it! *Ooooooh!* Let me just say this: If they know what they doing, you can come from getting your ass licked. He ain't never gotta touch your pussy!

ADELE: You know why? Cause the asshole and the pussy—they neighbors. It's all connected.

SOMMORE: You can lick it, you can chew on it, you can throw whipped cream and peanut butter and every muthafucking thing else, but I'm a look at your ass differently in the morning.

MO'NIQUE: See, I guess when you're married it's a different thing. When you're married it's like no muthafuckin' holds barred.

SOMMORE: I can get tied up, I can do all that shit. I love come. You can come all over me, I don't give a fuck. I prefer if you take your dick out, take the rubber off and come on my ass, come on my titties, come on my face. You can do whatever, it don't matter. But it's certain shit, like licking my ass, that I just ain't going with.

LOWBROW READER: What about a finger in the ass?

SOMMORE: No. A finger in the ass is cool, at times. But you gotta really have me there. And I love seeing a man jack his dick.

ADELE: Especially if you giving him a dance at the time, or some shit like that.

LAURA: If she didn't do nothing else, that little *Saved by the Bell* bitch in *Showgirls* worked that muthafuckin' lap dance. Goddamit!

MO'NIQUE: It fucked up her career, but she did her thing in *Showgirls.*

ADELE: She was bad. She made me say, "You know what? I need to brush up on my lap dancing."

LAURA: That bitch got down in that movie!

ADELE: You have to be into yourself, though. You got to turn yourself on when you doing your dance. You have to say, "I'm the shit right now!"

SOMMORE: And you gotta be spontaneous. Like, I love if we riding in the car, I'll get butt naked and suck his dick. I don't give a fuck. Just set it off! But I don't like having my ass licked and I don't like having my pussy ate.

LOWBROW READER: Do you believe that a dick can be too big?

MO'NIQUE: No. If you can push out a nine-pound baby, I don't believe there's a dick too big. I just don't.

SOMMORE: I ain't into real big dicks. I like nice size dicks. Once you start fucking a guy with a real big dick, you always gotta fuck guys with real big dicks. Then you become a size queen. You gotta go around auditioning muthafuckas to see if his dick's big. And I don't want no big pussy.

LAURA: I was with this guy before I was married and he had a real big dick. And I was on this gig—it was with Bernie Mac—and all of a sudden, right before the show, my uterus was flipping back. It can get knocked outta shape and when it comes back it's a painful muthafucka. Bernie and his road manager were like, "What is it? What can we do?" But I couldn't tell 'em I had fucked a nigga with a big dick and my uterus was flipping back!

SOMMORE: I ain't into no small dick, though. I don't even entertain that.

LAURA: A little dick can be okay because sometimes a little dick can hit that G-spot. It don't necessarily go all the way in but it's rubbing right at that little section, causing friction.

ADELE: I'm like Sommore. If your dick is too small, my favorite position is with another muthafucka. Come on, now. A little tiny dick is a waste of time. He need to get with an Asian woman. Does *Glamour* magazine use this kind of language?

Lowbrow Reader #3, 2003

DON KNOTTS:
A Salute to the Reluctant Hero

by Neil Michael Hagerty

THE FACE OF Don Knotts is rubbery, but not in the sense that it can be reshaped into a variety of presences; he defies that. His face is soft pink putty, yet his features remain stark and memorably precise. His most famous expression, or take, is probably the look of surprised fear wherein he stretches back the muscles surrounding the eyes while seeming to expand the orbs considerably beyond their sockets. At the same time, he puckers his lips as if to kiss his sweet grandiose schemes farewell while allowing his prematurely languid jaw to quiver. It is a burn as primal as Jack Benny's—a comedian whom Knotts admires greatly and the demigod from whom Knotts descends.

Many times, this patented pose suggests a child trying to hold still for a family photograph: Knotts craning his neck forward as oblivious parents fuss with an enormous flash contraption and exhort their subject to hold that emotion just a bit longer. And Knotts always obliges with a perfect face, because it is his passionate and emotional peak. This is not to say he is limited. After all, the look could mean many things: resignation, jealousy, shock, useless solicitude, recognition of his own stupidity, mortification, confusion, epiphany, regret of false bravado. It all depended on what he saw.

His control of speaking style is amazing. I've seen only a few impersonators get it right, despite its familiarity. Although it is often gentle and nuanced with passive-aggressive hostility, it is mostly nervous, reedy and rushed, as if it needs to be that way in order to avoid an embarrassing stammer.

Remembering a classic Don Knotts phrase: It starts with what sounds like an intake of breath speaking a word that rises in pitch. As if frustrated by the effort of communication, there comes a pause. Then a failed attempt at modulation in timbre as he hears how ridiculous his own voice sounds, generally followed by a rush of the next phrase as he desperately trails off and relinquishes silence to someone who will be listened to.

I often thought Ronald Reagan had incorporated Knotts's vocal technique into his own empty art, removing all sense of irony by transposing it, machinelike, into his soulfully skeptical drone of false wisdom.

Apologies to Don Knotts and Christopher Marlowe, in that order

It lies not in our power to make him cool,
The Shakiest Gun, Mr. Chicken—cast as knave or fool.

Our age plays down delight in Barney's gaffe,
Denies the Apple Dumpling Gang triggered a laugh.

Hot Lead and Cold Feet can't be TiVo'd; basic cable TV
Rarely plays Mr. Limpid or Mayberry RFD.

An aficionado spends most of her time instead
Insisting: whenever you read this, Don Knotts can't be dead.

Think long on the Reluctant Astronaut, near forgot;
For who ever loved, that loved not Don Knotts?

—M. Sweeney Lawless

Mutterings are peppered throughout Don Knotts's conversations like little gasps of air taken by a man submerged in water with only his flabby lips and nose above the surface. Knotts seemed to want to hold his place in conversations this way: *Yep...sure...well,* drawled creakily as he is blithely lectured at or flattered.

And then there is his whine, like the overwhelmed whistle a person might give when confronting a problem so huge that it's absurd to contemplate any human either having created it or coping with it. Knotts always had the soft, surrendering whistle haunting his voice. If he was angry and inspired, he would run more energy through it and blurt out objections in the tumbling sharp yelps that he dreamed would demand absolute understanding and attention.

With consummate skill and discipline, Don Knotts created a perfect physical vehicle with which to reluctantly participate in any drama. This comedic simplicity also contains a deep memento of perseverance beyond any remote necessity that could resist the final facts of human aloneness and transform total disregard for purpose, intention and consequence into a stubborn act of bravery.

....

Jesse Donald Knotts was born in Morgantown, West Virginia, in 1924. It is said he was a sickly child and suffered from periodic bouts of depression.

Don Knotts is a decorated veteran of the Second World War. He was awarded the World War II Victory Medal, the Philippine Liberation Medal, the Asiatic-Pacific Campaign Medal (with four bronze service stars), the Army Good Conduct Medal, the Marksman Badge (with Carbine Bar) and an Honorable Service Lapel Pin. Roughly 12 percent of the American population served in the military during Don Knotts's day. In the Vietnam War, about 4.3 percent of the population served, while, during our own effectively privatized time, only 1 percent of the U.S. population has volunteered for the active-duty military.

Knotts graduated from West Virginia University in 1948 with a degree in theater. From 1953 to 1955, he had a regular role in the soap opera *Search for Tomorrow*. He began a recurring role as the Man on the Street for the "Man on the Street" interviews on *The Steve Allen Show* in 1956, playing a nervous, hyperactive man who was ill at ease about being on television.

Of course, Knotts is best known as Deputy Barney Fife on *The Andy Griffith Show*, a role that earned him five Emmy Awards. Nobody likes a nerd, but everyone loved Knotts's portrayal of the painfully hyperactive, weak and whiny fall guy Fife. In the Bravo Network's recent survey of the 100 Greatest Television Characters of All Time, Fife ranked thirty-sixth, just ahead of Marcus Welby and behind Lou Grant. Knotts left the series in 1965 to pursue a career in movies. The actor's biggest box-office success was Disney's *The Apple Dumpling Gang*, a 1975 film that also featured Tim Conway, Harry Morgan and Bill Bixby; it grossed $32 million.[1] Knotts returned to television in 1979 to create one more classic character, the garishly dressed and socially overwhelmed landlord Ralph Furley on *Three's Company*. He stayed until the show ended its run in 1984.

....

There is a cult of Pez dispensers and DeLoreans and Linux. There is a cult of Aunt Bea. Don Knotts, however, needs no cult—his comedic skill in reckoning the American chasm between personality and identity is vast. And yet many of us feel compelled to rise from time to time and introduce some new

---

[1] This is the plot of *The Apple Dumpling Gang*: In 19th-century Quake City, California, confirmed bachelor Bill Bixby becomes the guardian of three orphaned siblings. The children find a giant gold nugget after an earthquake. The gold nugget brings problems, however, so they decide to give it to two bumbling outlaws (Knotts and Conway). But first they must steal the nugget from the bank vault where it's being held for safekeeping.

Illustration by Alex Eben Meyer

understanding of his mastery, as if it has been missed or under-appreciated. That is surely the result of Knotts's profound and exemplary commitment to his craft.

The Reluctant Hero Pack DVD (Universal) contains four of Knotts's films. It is a very great collection. I myself prefer *The Love God?* (1969), because it deposits Knotts's character far afield into the swinging '60s, which isolates his style most drastically from the colorful sets and situations. It also utilizes Technicolor splendidly. I could watch any number of chickens crossing any number of roads for hours and hours in Technicolor.[2]

The Love God? was written and directed by Nat Hiken. The film follows one Abner Peacock (Knotts), publisher of *The Peacock*, a bird-watching magazine on the brink of bankruptcy. Desperate to stay afloat, Abner takes on new partners who will use his publication as a front to publish a sexy gentleman's magazine. Unbeknownst to Abner, the first issue sells over 40 million copies. Abner becomes the unwilling spokesman for First Amendment rights when he is put on trial for smut. His defense lawyer paints the chaste Abner as a champion of liberation and free speech. He is acquitted and swept up in adulation. Soon, the unwitting playboy settles into the iconic role of the swinging bachelor lifestyle, but love and honesty ultimately get the better of him.

In *The Love God?* there is also ample space to enjoy another element of Don Knotts's work that primarily corresponds to his films. There is always an acceptance that deus ex machina must play a large part in the proceedings of the narrative. But because Knotts's technique is so refined and the plots of his movies so contrived and convoluted, I enjoy the feeling that the *deus* is

---

[2] Filming by the Technicolor process involved using colored filters and beam splitters on multiple strips of specifically color-sensitive black-and-white film. Incoming light was filtered and slivered into green, blue and red components and reflected onto the corresponding film strip. When the film was printed, it was bleached to remove the silver and then soaked in a chromatically opposite dye. One clear strip of film was then brought into contact with each of the three colored strips to create a single print. It looks fucking amazing.

being delayed by boredom or that it is more interested in the social structures that Knotts's character passes through than in reaching down to resolve the story. Knotts seems to stumble through great circumstances and peril, as if he is simply waiting to get to the end of the line like the movie itself—but then realizes he must exert a plea for dignity through some tantrum or slapstick disaster that does not alter the programmed motivations of Knotts's character or expand the fated narrative. Assuming for himself the duties of deus ex machina, like the ancient gods hoisted down onto the stage, Knotts erupts and provides convenient distraction for drastic and unlikely plot developments to lurch forward. I always imagine that Knotts is merely pretending to need to learn the lessons he is being ruthlessly taught. He only wants to return to the beginnings of the story intact after cascading down various jagged cliffs of pointless agitation he'd have just as well avoided were it not his destiny to be occasionally swept up into the maw of a motion picture. Hence, the cult of Don Knotts.

·····················

In 2005, Andy Griffith was awarded the Presidential Medal of Freedom. The White House issued this statement:

> Andy Griffith is one of America's best-known and most beloved entertainers. He is a man of humor, integrity, and compassion. The United States honors Andy Griffith for demonstrating the finest qualities of our country and for a lifetime of memorable performances that have brought joy to millions of Americans of all ages.

The same year, the *National Examiner* published a story headlined "Don Knotts's Sad Last Days":

> The 81-year-old who made Barney Fife a household

name was heartbroken when his doctors forbade him from making a trip from his Beverly Hills home to his hometown of Morgantown, West Virginia, for a parade and film festival in his honor earlier this month.

Knotts never really made anything like Griffith's *A Face in the Crowd*—a movie of which I presume the White House is entirely unaware.[3] I was kind of depressed by the story of Knotts's failing health (he passed away this February), so I wrote a fantasy picture in which I wished he could appear. It was to co-star Debra Messing, Allen Iverson and maybe some old members of the National Lampoon Radio Hour....

THE RETURN OF THE RELUCTANT HERO

Knotts is the man who flew the plane that dropped the first atomic bomb on Japan. His grandson (Iverson) is a pilot who is training to deploy a new U.S. "secret weapon" which will strike the ultimate blow and win the War on Terror.

When an ambitious press agent for the Defense Department (Messing) finds out that Iverson is related to Knotts, she gets Iverson to help her enlist Knotts to travel the world on a PR mission in order to accelerate the funding and deployment of the "secret weapon." Iverson agrees to help because he is in love with Messing. Knotts at first demurs, but capitulates when he realizes it will help his grandson find true love.

Knotts leaves for the preposterous PR tour. Along the way he overhears some scientists saying that the "secret weapon" is

---

[3] *A Face in the Crowd* (1957), starring Andy Griffith, Patricia Neal and Walter Matthau, directed by Elia Kazan, written by Budd Schulberg. The movie follows the rise and fall of a "country" comedian, Larry "Lonesome" Rhodes. Lonesome is a hobo discovered in an Arkansas jail who rises from there to host his own television show and become a minion of right-wing political forces. In the end, the woman who discovered him and cynically abetted his stardom becomes so terrified that she exposes the true, bloodthirsty face of this amiable singing vagabond to the world.

totally unstable but is being rushed to deployment by an idiotic President (Chevy Chase?).

Finally, the weapon is complete and Knotts is on hand for the televised unveiling. Through a series of mishaps, he winds up aloft in the plane as it screams through the skies heading for the Middle East. Over the radio, panicked officials guide him through the plane's navigation and control systems. Even the President screams at him, telling him to hit his target and win the war one more time. In the confusion, someone lets slip that if the "secret weapon" is actually unleashed, it will create a chain reaction that will destroy all life on earth. Knotts gains control of the plane, but instead of returning to base or hitting the terrorist target, he guides it out of earth's atmosphere and detonates himself in outer space, thus saving mankind.

A cover-up is quickly launched by the White House, but the disillusioned Messing and Iverson steal away with the digital transcripts of the flight. They expose the plot. They are married, Messing runs for Senate and Don Knotts becomes hero to the world.

Lowbrow Reader #5, 2006

LETTER FROM THE EDITOR: THE RULES OF MARRIAGE

by Jay Ruttenberg

Here's one thing you probably never thought of: Let's say you are walking down the street and notice your wife walking toward you. Even if you saw her as recently as that morning, you can't just give a cursory head nod or a "how ya doing?," as you might if you encountered somebody from the office. You have to stop and chat. This holds true even when you run into each other near the apartment, or if you are late for an appointment.

Now and then, everybody forgets his or her spouse's birthday. After such a blunder, it's present time. But what to get? One gift to avoid is a Dalmatian that you pick up on your route home from work, particularly if you do not know whether or not your wife is an animal lover; moreover, if she is allergic to felines, it is a bad idea to buy a pet kitten for the Dalmatian, even if the dog seems lonely because your wife doesn't play with it enough. Another present you'll live to regret: A written pledge promising not to give European-style cheek-to-cheek kisses to everybody you meet at your wife's office Christmas party.

Let's look at Halloween. If your father-in-law succumbs to cancer in August, it is considered unbecoming to dress as his ghost, back from the grave and rearing to raise holy hell, come October 31. Furthermore, if you suddenly find yourself on the losing end of a shaving cream and egg showdown with local junior high school students, do not insist that your wife defend you by either staging a sneak attack or phoning the police and shrieking that her upstanding-citizen husband is being held the victim of a wanton hooligan assault.

There are good ways and bad ways to wake your spouse in the morning. Injudicious methods include loudly revisiting an argument you had the previous week because a witty retort

Illustration by John Mathias

came to you in a dream. Another unsuccessful way: Stomping around the bedroom chanting, "This is what democracy sounds like!" on the morning of a big protest march or mayoral primary. Smoother wake-ups include gently lifting your spouse's pillow from underneath her head and saying, "Hey! You're late!" or mimicking an alarm clock's *brrrrrnnng* sound.

If your child-rearing plans predominantly consist of buying DVDs of *The Cosby Show* and "letting Bill do the talking," it is best to keep mum about them. If you do decide to reveal such plans, it is unwise to do so while your wife is in the bathroom waiting to view the results of a home pregnancy test that you declined to go to the drug store and purchase yourself because it would have been embarrassing, and *The Daily Show* was on.

If you decide to experiment with vegetarianism, it is inadvisable to sit next to your mother-in-law at a Labor Day barbecue and make "mooing" sounds as she eats a hamburger. Similarly, if you are in the formative stages of a religious conversion, do not insist on eulogizing your spouse's great-aunt in a foreign tongue. This is especially not recommended if you have just started taking courses in the language a month prior to the funeral; if you were not specifically invited to participate in the ceremony; and if you never had the opportunity of meeting the great-aunt while she was alive.

When you are out walking with your wife and a passing homeless man makes a crass comment, do not flash him a knowing smile and chase him down with a dollar bill, even if he "has a point" about her rear end. Another tip regarding the destitute: While it is a nice gesture to give neighborhood vagabonds warm clothes for the winter months, try to avoid donating scarves that were knit and initialized for you by your wife's ailing Nana Carol.

"If you decide to commit suicide by hanging yourself, make sure to leave behind a note. Otherwise, everybody will think you were masturbating." That's a good piece of advice—but not one to give your wife's troubled nephew after being asked to speak with the teen at a family gathering where your mother-in-law is standing within earshot. On a related note, the fact that your mother-in-law angrily employs the f-word in a conversation does not give you a tacit green light to use the term "poontang" while chatting with her at a subsequent Sunday morning brunch.

Lowbrow Reader #5, 2006

CURB

by Shelley Berman

Having been here before, I arrive
with expectations, certainties of
unexpected good. Surprises;
of story, dimension and degree
and, on these premises,
fortune-finding of my own,
what fortunes I myself
have brought unknowing –
discovery – to know
only at the knowing, and to know
I will soon be who
I am by being someone else,
and to know
the attention here – the
essence, end and persistence
of intention here – is Laughter.

There is a rare collective habit
here of hands held out; uncommon
care, comfort, kindnesses and kisses;
coffee, sweets and guiding touches
on the arm. A word of help, of praise,
of ease, a joke, and I am smitten,
beholden in this place.

With Curb I learn
the possessive pronoun "THE":
THE dressing room, THE closet,
THE hanger, THE toilet.
My, my, I am My-deprived.
Isn't this an invasion of
THE privacy?

We are the Immaculate Exhalation,
envy of roses and nectar-drunk gods.
We are the breath-mint–addicted,
worshipful druids of chlorophyll,
confident of one-on-one kisses
and making close nose-to-nose gossip.
We are the Breath Unremarkable, and
if by some chance noticeable, it's
probably the mint. No one
here has need to fear the chance of
olfactory embarrassments. (This
solely addresses breath offense,
no guarantees re: flatulence.)

Newton's Law in Malibu:
An Actor at rest tends to stay
at rest and an Actor in motion
tends to stay in motion with
the same speed and in the same
direction unless acted upon
by Another Force.

The Other Force:
His glasses ride
haughty on a high-ridged nose,
his gray fringe fits
like a loose tiara slipped down
round the ears, the gray
giving way to darker-hued
rosettes clinging in ignored
desperation to the nape.
Opposite the nape,
a smart smile, appealing
though shockingly revealing
of wondrously perfect teeth.
The Other Force. He
knows where he goes, we go
where he goes where
we go.

Craft-critical is the Trust:
Improvisation. This is
where the doings emerge,
where the Taking
is the Giving, where we
become the symbiotic paradigm,
where we in our invention
are mindful always of
the end and persistence
of intention –
the Laughter, the Laughter.
The end is nothing
if not the end in Laughter.

Lowbrow Reader #7, 2009

Illustration by Mike Reddy

THE COMEDIAN JIM MACGEORGE
by Shelley Berman

He comes to us aslant, like a man
uninvited, a good ear forward, lolling eyes
downward, a mouth at ease in a distantly
remembered smile. He stands to hear
his turn, drooping like a sunflower.

By the velour he walks his wait, turning
in the draping dark: to here, to there and back,
as if chasing down his whispers, as if prying
upon himself, as if dancing to last night's laughter.
Now, abruptly he is still, and he braces to hear
his name.

He goes to the light, to the stage, as if without
intention, as if wary of the floor, as if weighing
a knock on a door so as to sell a brush
bravely while hoping there is no answer.
Yet, with wise eyes beading, he is opening
his case.

Lines crack like Astaire's torpedoes, cannonades
of sudden laughter; the stage is a jubilant
realm as he peoples his court with kings' voices,
with each jut of the jaw or the lip, new face after
face familiar. Now, shuffling with foxy grace,
he smiles to his applause.

He comes off as a man home from work, seeking
a place for his cap; his still lolling eyes held wide,
surprised by the grip of new darkness. In the quiet
he loosens his waist, perhaps ponders
a moment that failed, then, recalling his
laughter he stands, drooping like a sunflower.

Illustration by Mike Reddy

WHAT TO DO WITH OUR CEOs?

Illustrations by Mike Reddy

America has a CEO problem! Executive salaries are running wild, and the gap between the super-rich and everybody else is growing larger by the day. Nonplussed, in 2008, Lowbrow *turned to our nation's funnymen with the question of our time: What should be done with our nation's CEOs?*

PATTON OSWALT
Comedian

The answer is simple. We need to triple, quadruple, sextuple their salaries. At their current pay level, the most we can hope for from CEOs is slightly profane behavior and garish houses.

But imagine railroad baron–level fortunes, Caligula-strength immunity from any behavior consequences. The only way to destroy this tumor is to feed it until it explodes.

I don't want a CEO who can get away with having a mistress and a private jet. I want them hollowing out private islands and creating subterranean combat cultures, full of trained hobos and Russian mail-order brides, breeding battalions of sunlight-deprived berserkers to get back at the swim-team captain from high school who swirlied them at summer camp. I want them burning their names, continent-sized, on the surface of Mars.

Plus, the rebound guilt will go toward creating bizarre philanthropies—literacy courses for reptiles, cupcake walls between Israel and Palestine, and community hooker banks. I'm past worrying about the world being shitty—I just don't want it to be boring.

ROB HUEBEL
Comedian, Human Giant

I think CEOs should be forced to go and live for one month a year with their lowest paid employee. That way they could get a feel for what it's like to struggle as a working family in this country. Wait. This is a great idea for a reality show. Oh shit. Don't steal my idea. It's called "Fortune 500 on the Futon." Just a bunch of old white guys sleeping over and trying to scrape by with a low-income family. And in the last episode, the family gets to kill and eat them.

JOHN WATERS
Director

They should all be given big raises so they can buy confrontational contemporary art and finance weirdo underground movies.

JUSTIN BOND
Performer and "Flaming Creature," Kiki and Herb

Since most of them are old, white, fat and suffering from compromised colons—cancer, diverticulitis—it wouldn't be very practical to give them anything to do that would be too rigorous. They would probably be most useful either on their hands and knees or bent over something. I'm thinking that so many people have been running around catering to their unreasonable demands and expectations for so long that a lot of us have sore and calloused feet. The best thing we could do, then, is to put them to work in nail salons across the country. I think it would probably take two CEOs per person—one for each foot. Every exploited worker should get fifteen minutes on a massage chair with each foot up the ass of a "retired" CEO. That should be just enough time to exfoliate and soften even the most over-exploited worker's tired and careworn feet. Maybe it would even ease the dreaded "Restless Legs Syndrome."

MICHAEL J. ROSEN
Writer, Former Thurber House Director

Abraham Maslow, father of self-actualization, once said that if the only tool you possess is a hammer, everything begins to look like a nail. Actually, it can't require much fatherly stature to suggest that hammer-headed CEOs everywhere have a screw loose! They need other tools to appreciate the human machinery that floats their boat on a sea of wealth.

In lieu of a $450/hour session with the too-late psychologist, I'd recommend that for every extra digit that a CEO's salary exceeds the lowest paid employee in his or her company, the CEO spend one quarterly earning period contemplating company operations not as a metaphorical hammer, but as one of the following tools: a dandelion weeder, a saws-all, a fistful of extra-fine steel wool, an oyster-shucking knife, a table crumber, a pair of extra-small latex gloves, or a staple remover. The real challenge, of course, as "things" begin to look a little different, is how to use such personal transformations to create lasting corporate change, inspiration in the workplace, increased profits—and still manage a little insider trading.

GEORGE SAUNDERS
Writer

I don't really know what else we can do with them, other than praise them—for their excellent accomplishments, their positive attitudes, and their ability to, by skillfully working within the system, build a better world—for themselves, yes, but also for us. I think we should especially praise those who aren't very good at it; the ones who go from corporation to corporation, leaving them just as they were, or even running them slightly into the ground, all the while collecting huge salaries and bonus packages, until finally they really screw one up and are fired, at which time they get rich again by writing a "how to succeed" book. We should also praise them for being smart enough to earn up to 50 times what their average worker is making. You think that's easy? You try it! My average worker, "Mo," makes $10 an hour. Which means I would have to make $500 an hour to be as smart as the average CEO. Which, guess what? I don't. I am doing this interview right now, answering this question: for free. So who's the idiot, me or your average CEO? I'll tell you who: Me. "Mo" agrees. "Mo," what are you doing, reading over my shoulder when you're supposed to be fanning me? I may have to cut your pay. Ha, ha, just kidding. Put down the cudgel. Go trim the sheep, "Mo," I don't want to get into a big thing with you.

RANDY NEWMAN
Songwriter

I'm writing a song about it. I think that will solve the problem.
I did the first Farm Aid and the farm problem cleared up. I've
written songs about civil rights and no one even *mentions* that
issue anymore.

BILLY MADISON:
A Love Letter

by Jay Ruttenberg

I HAVE HEARD it said that it's during times of emotional tumult that young men are drawn to Bob Dylan, or at least to religion. Yet it was under such a cloud that, one summer in the 1990s, I grew suddenly and undyingly gripped by a very different tour de force: *Billy Madison*, the 1995 movie featuring Adam Sandler in his first real star turn. Over a decade later, I stand convinced that few American comedies are funnier—and none as critically undervalued. "We were trying to make a movie that critics didn't like," the film's director, Tamra Davis, would later tell me. "We were trying to make a movie for us and for kids—a movie that insulted adults and made them mad." *Billy Madison* was a work that would instigate me to return to the theater, year in, year out, to see Adam Sandler's subsequent films— some inspired, some formulaic, but all inferior to the debut— and reevaluate my own taste in popular culture. It would draw me uncharacteristically close to my brother while pushing me away from those who mindlessly dismissed "low" art. Mostly, the movie would make me laugh time and again, a familiar joke that blooms with every telling.

Outside of the eternal problem of being a spoiled brat just north of 20 years old—that embarrassingly self-indulgent age when the world effectively functions as one's mirror—it is unclear exactly what was afflicting me at the time I encountered the film. Marooned at my parents' home in suburban Chicago, my friends and life were back east. I was withdrawn and temperamental, finding myself spending an unhealthy amount of time with the family poodles; over the course of the summer, the dogs began to subtly shun me for more engaging social commitments.

One evening, I successfully lured the poodles to the basement with a tennis ball only to encounter an unwelcome surprise: my little brother and an army of his friends, none older than 14. My parents' rec room resembled the set of a Sherlock Holmes movie, such was the fog of marijuana that engulfed it. I turned to leave, but it was too late. "Hey!" one of the aspiring deviants cried out. "For once in your life, will you buy us beer?"

"No, I'm, uh, er," I said. "No."

"Want some weed?" another inquired.

"No, thanks."

"Come on!" he protested. I hesitated, wondering what it would be like to succumb to peer pressure from a 4-foot-5 boy with a squeaky voice.

"That's okay," I finally said. "What are you guys up to?"

"We're gonna watch *Billy Madison*!" my brother exclaimed. "It's the funniest fucking movie ever. Want to watch with us?"

"Hmmm," I said.

"Billy! Billy! Billy!" the boys chanted.

"I don't know," I said.

As appealing as the prospect of going upstairs to my childhood bedroom and staring at the wall seemed, I was tempted by their mocking plea. I had long admired Adam Sandler. I was in high school when he joined the cast of *Saturday Night Live*, in 1991; a young-looking 25-year-old with Jewish hair and oversized flannel shirts, he was one of the first television stars who seemed like somebody I might have known. He was fratty and hostile yet peculiar and good-hearted—the comic reminded me of my brother—and his work had an undeniable arty streak. He reveled in an inspired dumbness. His best material—a sketch in

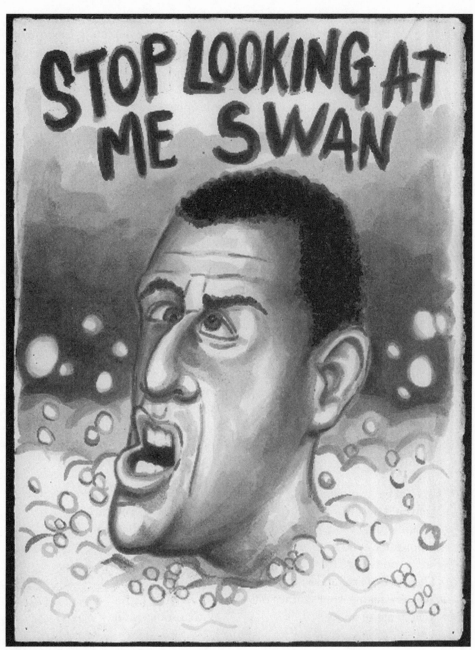

Illustration by Tom Sanford

which Sandler, with Chris Farley, pleads with an unseen man to let Sandler take care of a dog; a silent piece depicting a simpleton struggling to cross a city street; and, most famously, the ostensibly amateurish bits he performed on "Weekend Update"— appeared the work of a madman. Like most novel televised comedy, his material's inherent appeal was that it seemed not to belong on television at all.

During my first semester of college, Sandler released his debut album of sketches and songs, *They're All Gonna Laugh at You!* This 1993 CD was stranger still, and had the added advan-

---

WHEN WE TWO PARTIED
with abject apologies to Lord Byron
by M. Sweeney Lawless

It's true, when we met
My father had paid
For me to repeat 1st
All the way through 12th grade.
Your term was "pathetic"
On the grade-school front lawn,
But I still had high hopes of us
Getting it on.

I should have known
We would never be wed.
"No milk will ever
Be our milk," you said.
But not too long after
(The reasons are muddy),
You were taking your clothes off
To help me to study.

I'll think of your heiney
When I'm lonely at night
And I'm staging a shampoo-
Conditioner fight.
When I showed you my tent
With Porta-John plumbing
Did the porn make you wonder
If you had been slumming?

Did the penguin say something?
I thought that you cared
For the man who groped you
On a bus (double-dared).
If I should meet thee
In some public place
How should I greet thee?
With a squirt smiley face.

tage of being unspeakably filthy. My dorm-mates and I listened incessantly at the expense of other activities, like going to class or meeting girls.

So when *Billy Madison*, Sandler's big cinematic unveiling, came out a mere two years later, did I see it? Of course not! By then, my friends and I had moved on to what we perceived as cooler ground: old soul music, increasingly obscure indie-rock bands, film noir. Besides, the movie looked inane. The premise—a wealthy slacker must repeat grades 1-through-12 in order to take over his father's Fortune 500 hotel chain!—seemed precisely the type of cynical Hollywood drivel that for decades had neutered promising comedians. The marketing campaign revolved around an irritating photograph of Sandler squeezed into a tiny desk, a scolding teacher with model proportions at his side. Critics either ignored or maligned the movie. "If you've seen the trailer," the *Washington Post* reported, "you're one up on those of us who have endured the entire film." I had seen the trailer. It included a skidding record needle, a Jackson 5 song and scenes of Sandler wooing the comely teacher.

"Billy! Billy! Billy!" my brother's freshly bar mitzvahed friends chanted.

"Come on, watch it, asshole."

"It's so funny!"

"Okay," I said. "I'll watch the damn thing. Just shut up already."

....

Billy Madison opens with Adam Sandler, as the titular protagonist, lying on a pool lounger, floating in an opulent fountain fit for Versailles. He wears shorts, shoes and a baseball cap, a daiquiri at his side, and serenades a bottle of suntan lotion. "Oh, the sun tries to burn me," he affectionately informs the bottle. "But you won't let it—will ya?" It is not immediately clear whether the character is drunk, woozy from sun, mentally retarded or just downright weird. As the opening credits roll, he realizes that it is "nudie magazine day" and races to the mailbox to unwrap a package of demented periodicals, each cover seemingly torn from *MAD* magazine. Hallucinating, Billy spots what he believes is a giant penguin, which he proceeds to chase through the estate's immaculately landscaped grounds.

In my parents' basement, I stood to leave. "This is the stupidest thing I've ever seen," I grumbled. "I'm going upstairs."

"Come on, don't be a dick," my brother said.

"I'll give it five more minutes," I reasoned. "But that's all."

Yet as the movie rolled on, I grew more and more acclimated to its strange tone. Before my allotted five minutes were up, Billy had entered a formal dinner, presided over by his father and featuring an array of suit-clad businessmen. Sandler throws himself into the lavish dining room with all the chutzpah of Groucho Marx, hunched shoulders and all. In short order, he slurps soup, tells his yuppie nemesis to shut up, unleashes a torrent of gibberish and—effortlessly switching from Groucho to Harpo—gnaws on the arm of an elderly businessman. I was intrigued. The movie seemed anarchic in a manner generally eschewed by modern Hollywood. As in *Pee-wee's Big Adventure* and the Marx Brothers' Paramount films, the adult world was depicted as a cartoonish joke where dreams go to die. Against it stood a maniac man-child, alone yet fearless, eager to disrupt the stiffs who surrounded him. As an immature 20-year-old hesitantly eyeing a post-college gulf that was approaching with terrifying speed, I was oddly moved.

The movie never relented. Its every scene proved some strange jewel. Billy and his layabout buddies, played by the comedian Norm MacDonald and the hefty actor Mark Beltzman (in a role originally intended for Sandler regular Allen Covert), burn a bag of dog excrement on an elderly man's porch. After the old man, resplendent in white underwear and boots, stomped out the fire, my brother and his friends shouted along with Sandler's flabbergasted line: "He called the shit 'poop'!" When

Chris Farley appeared, perpetually red-faced in a spectacular extended cameo, the boys all but cheered. With each passing scene, I edged away from the door and closer to the 14-year-olds.

By the end of the week, I had watched the picture four times. My brother and I walked around the house swapping lines from the film in place of our usual insults. I phoned friends back in Boston and New York, breathlessly imploring them to watch *Billy Madison*, ideally with junior high school students. I screened the VHS tape for my poodles (who did not appreciate it) and my parents (who did). "Billy is so sweet," my mother said.

It galled me that I had grown so snotty as to have turned up my nose at this movie when it was in theaters. Even less excusable was the fact that the country's cultural gate-keepers had uniformly snubbed it. As my brother's bleary-eyed friends recognized but every working film critic in America somehow missed, *Billy Madison* was a smart picture flagrantly poking out from a dumb exterior. Although the movie never stoops to the knee-jerk irony that by the mid-'90s was creeping into American entertainment, the filmmakers treat its sole weakness—the high-concept *Back to School* plot—at a remove. When the protagonist first proposes to his father that he return to school for 24 weeks in order to take over a company, Sandler all but winks at his audience. "That's some idea—you just think of that?" Billy's gruff father, played by Darren McGavin, asks him.

"Yeah, I did," Billy replies. "It's pretty good, huh?" Then, left alone onscreen, Sandler dances for the camera.

The world is full of comedies that begin with a flourish and gradually lose their nerve, caving to the pedestrian demands of plot and character development. Though it abides by Hollywood's customary story patterns—its emotional turning point occurs when Billy pretends to urinate in his pants—*Billy Madison* never blinks. At its conclusion, in a much-loved scene featuring the titanic *Saturday Night Live* writer James Downey, the film upends its plot while driving it to conclusion. The scene falls as part of a plot twist in which Billy dispenses with his original plan in favor of an "academic decathlon" pitting him against his rival (a beautifully depraved Bradley Whitford). The two men stand onstage before the cheering Knibb High audience; Downey's poker-faced principal serves as judge and jury. Faced with a difficult question, Billy scans the audience and spots the first-grade teacher from the beginning of his quest. Emboldened, he gives a rousing response, citing the simple truths he had learned from her. The crowd bursts into applause.

This is the point in most comedies, including the 20 subsequent films to star Adam Sandler, in which sentimentality trumps humor and a tidy conclusion rears its head. Instead, *Billy Madison* falls off the rails. "Mr. Madison," Downey's principal dryly states:

> "What you've just said is one of the most insanely idiotic things I have ever heard. At no point in your rambling, incoherent response were you even close to anything that could be considered a rational thought. Everyone in this room is now dumber for having listened to it. I award you no points, and may God have mercy on your soul."

In later years, this speech became the type of bit that gets replayed ad nauseam on YouTube, often intercut with unrelated cultural ephemera. In the context of the film itself, the speech is genuinely shocking— the opposite of a viewer's expectations at the closing stages of a movie already loaded with such twists. It is the pivotal scene of *Billy Madison*, and arguably the funniest. A decade and a half after watching it, the image of my brother and his young friends hooting and hollering remains planted in my mind, a fond memory to drive away the blues. Watching it in the basement, I laughed louder than I had all summer.

....

Tamra Davis was not Sandler's first choice to direct *Billy Madison*. "I had done *CB4* for Universal and we all had a good experience," Davis tells me, sitting at a Tribeca Le Pain Quotidien in the fall of 2009. "They were making this movie with Adam Sandler—another starring vehicle. The studio wanted me to direct the movie, so they flew me to New York to meet with Adam. I didn't know him at all personally, just from *Saturday Night Live*. We got along really well, but then I found out that I didn't get the job. He ended up hiring a friend of his— somebody within the group that he was working with."

Sandler, who had scripted *Billy Madison* with his old NYU roommate (and *Saturday Night Live* writing cohort) Tim Herlihy, persuaded Universal to tap an untested director: Stephen Kessler, who had given the comedian a commercial part early in Sandler's career. Around the same time, Davis was hired by a different studio to helm *Bad Girls*, a western that she was working on with Drew Barrymore.

Bad Girls started life auspiciously: a return to indie film for the young director, whose acclaimed first feature (1993's low-budget *Guncrazy*) had starred Barrymore, as well. Originally intended for New Line, *Bad Girls* was sold to 20th Century Fox as it was being developed.

"It was a typical situation where a movie was an indie, then all of a sudden became a studio movie," Davis says. Fox "had a different movie in mind than the film I was making. It came out in the press that I was trying to make a 'feminist western'—and so what if I was?" Davis shot nine days of *Bad Girls* before being taken off the picture. The tacky movie created by her successor, disparaged by Barrymore herself, has been forgotten to time.

Meanwhile, outside Toronto, Kessler had started shooting *Billy Madison*. At home nursing her emotional wounds from having been fired, Davis received a surprising call from Universal. "*Billy Madison* was becoming a disaster," she recounts. "The studio wasn't happy, Adam wasn't funny and they were behind on schedule. They asked if I would come out and finish the picture. I went from thinking, 'Oh my God, I'll never work again' to 'Gosh, now *I'm* the one who's replacing somebody else.' In a way, it's this confidence, or craziness, that defines a director."

Universal fired Kessler on a Thursday, after a mere three days of shooting. The same day, in a histrionic scenario that seems torn from *Entourage*, Davis flew into Toronto with the studio's president; she began shooting Monday morning. For years afterward, whenever Davis dropped by a set, her friends jokingly would say: "Uh-oh." At the time, however, she was received with enthusiasm. "When you're a director, you're a leader," she reasons. "A dispirited crew is a wonderful crew to get. You walk in and save the day."

If for Davis, picking up *Billy Madison* represented an opportunity to rebound from the disappointments of *Bad Girls*, for Sandler her entrance provided a true eleventh-hour opportunity. The comedian was between seasons at *Saturday Night Live*, where he ranked among a handful of young stars on the rise. His future as a Hollywood box-office gorilla was hardly a foregone conclusion: The handful of minor film roles he had completed were undistinguished and *Saturday Night Live* was being battered in the press. (In 1995, the year of *Billy Madison*'s release, he would be fired from the show, along with Farley.) Moreover, *Billy Madison* was Sandler's baby: a culmination of the aesthetic he had mined on television and record, with a script he had labored over with his old friend Herlihy. "Billy's the closest I've come to playing myself," Sandler told an *Entertainment Weekly* reporter visiting the movie's set. "I feel so much pressure because I want it to be as good as it can be."

He was tanking. The few scenes shot by Kessler that survive to the finished movie are incongruously gloomy and oddly paced. Under the stress, Sandler had pulled a neck muscle and was having trouble turning his head—not the ideal attribute for a leading man. "He knew he was in trouble," Davis says. "This was his big shot. What was going on wasn't necessarily his fault—the director was blamed—but he had to get it together.

"It was like survival," she continues. "Adam and I had to *quickly* develop a relationship and make the funniest, greatest movie ever. We created this little circle of me, Adam and Tim Herlihy. We had to work weekends, nighttime, whenever. Because I had no prep. I had to all of a sudden walk onto a movie that I didn't know anything about."

At night, Sandler would phone Davis, hotel room to hotel room, to discuss the next day's scenes, at times describing to the director what was funny about a particular joke. Davis made immediate visual tweaks to the movie, tidying characters' clothing and even lengthening the skirt of the female lead (Bridgette Wilson, 1990's Miss Teen USA and the future wife of serve-and-volley artist Pete Sampras). She kept an eye on what Sandler ate so that he would stay trim. (A screen comedian must be fit or fat; doughiness just looks schlumpy.) Davis also flushed the set with color. A rainbow vividness runs through much of her work, but the bright tones seem particularly indispensable to *Billy Madison*, casting the picture in a cartoon glow that amplifies and even sanctions the comedy's surrealism. And for a movie set among grade-school students, overstated color proved a natural fit.

Perhaps most significantly, Davis strived to move the film quickly and provide the congenial atmosphere that had been missing at the start of the shoot. "I knew instinctively that if you're working on a comedy, you have to have fun," she says. "If I have a grip who's in a bad mood or just cursed—that's not allowed. The actor has to feel like when he walks on that set, everybody is there to laugh at him."

....

Billy Madison is not a director-driven movie. Its producer, Robert Simonds—a juvenilia specialist who produced all of Sandler's movies through 2000's rip-roaringly demented *Little Nicky*—is known for creating star-friendly farces, retaining directors as afterthoughts. "In the TV business directors are more interchangeable because it's built all around Seinfeld or Roseanne or Drew Carey," Simonds told *New York Times* reporter Bernard Weinraub in 1998. "My movies are along those lines. An Adam Sandler movie is all Adam Sandler." *Billy Madison* is patently the vision of Sandler and Herlihy. No other screenwriters could have spun these jokes, just as no other actor could have delivered them convincingly.

Yet in Tamra Davis, his relief pitcher, the comedian happened upon an ideal collaborator. More versatile than most of his directors, she has piloted populist comedies, critically besmirched indie films, documentaries, music videos and sitcoms. While never curtailing Sandler's lowbrow inclinations, she brought to the film a distinctive visual perspective that's generally lacking in such movies. A decade later, Judd Apatow— Sandler's pre-fame roommate who visited him on set—would grow famous for encouraging his actors to improvise lines. In *Billy Madison*, Davis, too, would shoot from the script, then ask the comic to ad-lib a wilder take—resulting, for instance, in a scene depicting Billy yelling at an ornamental swan while he takes a bubble bath.

Davis is a fascinating, slightly understated figure. Her career is full of the stylistic twists and turns with which an artist avoids getting pigeonholed, but at the same time can escape acclamation. She directed the debut starring vehicles of the three sharpest comedy minds of their generation: Chris Rock (1993's *CB4*), Dave Chappelle (1998's *Half Baked*) and, of course, Sandler. Her MTV work consists of a string of Sonic Youth videos from the band's early Geffen years (including "100%," co-directed with a young Spike Jonze) as well as Hanson's "MMMBop." Most recently, she directed *Jean-Michel Basquiat: The Radiant Child*, a documentary that includes rare footage of the late painter that Davis herself shot in 1986; the filmmaker's early admiration for the artist presages the bright colors that pulsate through her own work. Davis also produces a homespun web show, tamradaviscookingshow.com, in which the director demonstrates the veggie snacks that she and her husband—Michael Diamond, the Beastie Boy—make for their two kids. (As Davis speaks of *Billy Madison*, Diamond and one of the couple's doll-like sons stop by Le Pain Quotidien, the latter smartly swiping a cookie straight off his mother's plate.) The family lives in downtown Manhattan and Malibu; the grown-up half shares the fantastically rare ability to create chic art that can stimulate a broad audience.

Davis is one of the few female directors to penetrate mainstream Hollywood. Women tend to make superior interviewers to their male counterparts—where her competitors talked, Oprah listened—and one wonders how other comedies would pan out were they fueled by less testosterone. "It was important to let Adam be Adam," Davis says. "I think it was Chris Rock who told me, 'If there's a joke under the table, you get the camera under the table—I'll tell the joke.' It was best for me to not be the 30-year-old girl I was at the moment, because I wasn't the audience. I had to become a 14-year-old boy and not put my judgment on it."

In shooting *Billy Madison*, Davis found herself engulfed in funnymen, many on summer leave from *SNL*. Yet perhaps unbeknownst to her cast and crew, it was the director who had the comedic pedigree. "My grandfather, Stan Davis, was a big comedy writer," she explains. "He started out in Chicago—he wrote for the Blondie and Dagwood comic strip—and moved to Hollywood, where my grandmother was under contract as a dancer at Fox. The story goes that he was making his living as a tailor, and would put his jokes in the pockets of coats. All the comedians started coming to him, because he had the best jokes. He became one of the big writers of one-liners. My grandfather wrote for all the comedians, mayors, presidents. If you were Ronald Reagan and you were going to talk in front of the firemen, you would call Stan Davis and he'd give you a couple fireman jokes.

"I grew up in Hollywood," Davis continues. "My grand-parents had a house on La Cienega and Sunset, and there were comedians around all the time. Bob Hope, Sammy Davis Jr.... Milton Berle really was like Uncle Miltie. My grandfather wasn't a 'funny guy.' If anything, he was kind of grumpy. But as a kid, you didn't realize that that was his sarcasm. He would constantly be writing jokes on yellow legal pads—he knew all the formulas. When I was a little kid, my first job was typing them up on three-by-five index cards and filing the jokes for him. Later, when I went to film school, I lived in his basement. It was a little cellar where he used to write and was filled with eight-by-tens of my grandfather with famous celebrities, like what you'd see at a deli. He had all these card catalogues filled with one-liners, from A-to-Z. When I was a punk-rock kid, people would come over, get high and pull out these three-by-five cards with these ridiculous jokes."

Even before abandoning tailoring, Stanley Davis would write for Groucho Marx, Jimmy Durante, Redd Foxx, Hope and Berle; upon his death in 1982, the *Times* reported that five min-utes of his material typically sold for $1,000. "In a sense, I *did* have a comedy background," Tamra Davis says. "It just came in a very different way [than Sandler]. I had respect—which is probably the best thing to have. When you respect the come-dian, you do whatever you can to let them be funny."

Directing Rock in *CB4*, Davis encountered a hardened standup accustomed to fishing for laughs; Sandler, Rock's one-time *SNL* office-mate, proved more elusive. "Chris would be standing there at seven in the morning with a plate of waffles, already trying to make me laugh," Davis says. "Adam kept me on my toes a bit more: Okay, how's he feeling this morning? Did he sleep well? How do we make him funny today?" At the same time, Sandler showed an astonishing command of screen humor. Often, before shooting a scene, the star would pull his director aside and tell her how an actor's line should sound; then Davis would attempt to coax the same reading from the actors, without letting on that the phrasing was coming from Sandler. (Such mimicry is easier to elicit from child actors than grown-up ones, Davis explains.)

Sandler would stop at little, it seemed, for a laugh. "I learned a lot," Davis says. "For example, hurting kids is funny. Adam called me up and said, 'Tamra, tomorrow we're shooting the dodgeball scene. I'm really gonna hit those kids.' I said, 'You can't do that.' But he said, 'No—I'm serious. Get the balls there and find out which kid wants to get hit.'" The ensuing scene, depicting Billy beaning first-graders to the tune of "Beat on the Brat," is hilarious in its brutality. "Those kids got hit *hard*," Davis recalls. "I cut before the tears."

Upon the film's release, the scene was singled out as "dismal" by a curmudgeonly Siskel & Ebert.

....

As with many Hollywood movies made on modest budgets, *Billy Madison* was shot in the Toronto area: The Madison mansion is actually the Parkwood Estate, where Colonel R. Samuel McLaughlin, the founder of the McLaughlin Motor Car Company, moved in 1917. The auto baron's ostentatious home, built into the Jazz Age, further links the picture to the Marx Brothers movies of yore. One almost expects Billy to court not Bridgette Wilson, but Margaret Dumont.

Concurrently to *Billy Madison*, another comedy about a callow rich kid aiming to inherit his father's company was shooting in Canada: *Tommy Boy*, which starred Sandler's fellow *SNL* cast-members David Spade and Chris Farley, the latter of whom also held a small role as *Billy Madison*'s aggrieved school-bus driver. The stars from both films stayed in the same Toronto hotel. Upon hearing this information, an unworldly teen-age boy might imagine that the comedians were in a constant state of madness, plotting outlandish jokes through the night.

Improbably, he would be correct. Sandler and Herlihy took to carrying around a cassette recorder so they could tape people and mock their words, like Andy Warhol gone junior high. Often, the pair would tell the same joke—first Herlihy, then, in a funny voice, Sandler. One time, a nude Chris Farley emerged from the double doors that opened onto Sandler's hotel room, dancing with his penis tucked between his legs. And the whole group took to playing "the Dead Game," in which everybody in Sandler's hotel room would close their eyes while one person faked his own death scene. "In one of the games, we opened our eyes and Farley was lying in front of us, naked with an Evian bottle sticking out of his ass," Davis recalls. "It was scary to see how far Sandler and Farley would go for a laugh."

In filming his brilliant handful of *Billy Madison* scenes, Farley—who would die of a heart attack in 1997—was equally extreme, albeit less blue. "Before Farley did his scenes," Davis says, "he would line up six or seven shots of espresso, down them right in front of me and then get on that bus. Then, he would hold his breath until he became, like, purple. I was watching this on a monitor—hiding in the back of the bus or in a travel vehicle—and I honestly thought he was going to have a heart attack. Meanwhile, Adam and Herlihy were laughing *hysterically*. It was always on the edge of going too far, which was the brilliance of Chris Farley. He pushed you so far to the edge that you were constantly concerned. She's nervous thinking you're going to kill yourself? That's comedy."

Another *Saturday Night Live* hand up north that summer was Jim Downey, who was helping Fred Wolf with *Tommy Boy*'s script. Downey has been a writer at *SNL* intermittently since 1976; responsible for many of the show's political sketches, he is a man who arguably has helped swing presidential elections. Sandler and Herlihy revered him. The respect was mutual. "Adam was the closest thing [*SNL*] ever had to Jerry Lewis," Downey tells me. "And I mean that in a totally good way. He was a really strong, eccentric character who was more of a personality than an ensemble player. There were certain things that he brought to the show that we had never had before and haven't had since."

Downey is not an actor in the traditional sense. His CV predominantly consists of stoic, mildly creepy bit parts on *SNL* and, strangely, Paul Thomas Anderson's Oscar-winning 2007 film *There Will Be Blood*. Yet when Sandler asked him to play *Billy Madison*'s principal, he readily agreed; like Davis, Downey found himself on set within days. Although Sandler and Herlihy had written the character, it was Downey who crafted the principal's climactic speech. "The origin of that speech was when Farley would talk at writers' meetings," Downey says. "I would go, 'Thanks, Chris—everyone in the room is now dumber. I hope you're proud of yourself.'" Though he's on-screen for a matter of minutes, Downey's every utterance is unsettling and memorable. "That speech has probably been seen by more people than anything else I've ever been in or written," he says. "One time, I took a train to visit a friend of mine in New Jersey. His son had three friends over, and they all turned out to meet my train— it was like Lenin returning to Finland Station. They couldn't believe that I was there in the flesh: the principal from *Billy Madison*."

Downey's principal is one of many smaller characters in *Billy Madison* to rise above their call of duty. Bradley Whitford plays the film's stock villain as a conniving rogue, so wicked he reads almost as a parody of such a figure. "That's one of the funniest bad guys you'll ever see," Downey says. "His performance was so intense and crazy. It shows what a good actor can do in a part that otherwise might not be memorable." (Whitford would go on to star in Aaron Sorkin's *The West Wing* as well as the short-lived *Studio 60 on the Sunset Strip*, in which he portrayed the producer of a *SNL*-like show.) Steve Buscemi, a frequent Sandler player who had co-starred with him in 1994's *Airheads* but remains identified with artier fare, appears briefly, in lipstick. Josh Mostel, son of Zero, gives an oddly poignant performance as a sniveling grade-school principal. And Norm MacDonald, generally hamstrung in acting roles, somehow seems at home as Billy's drunken friend. "When I read the script, it mentioned Billy and his buddy," Davis says. "But when I got there, it's this *crazy* guy Norm MacDonald. He was like Gary Cooper or something. I said, 'Adam, this guy is...old.' He was like, 'Yeah—that's the funny part.'"

At Le Pain Quotidien, Davis laughs fondly. "We had *so* much fun when we made that movie," she says. "It was their [group's] good times. Nobody had failed. Nobody had any big successes. Everyone was on the rise. There was no depression and no sadness. It was an amazing, amazing time."

....

Billy Madison ended production with a flourish. Upon returning to California, the director found her collaboration with the actor continued, as Sandler—perhaps protective of his masterwork's evolution, perhaps still mindful of a director who hailed from outside his circle—joined her for much of the editing process. Although such involvement is unusual for a star, Davis welcomed it. "By that time, Adam and I were like best friends," she says. "He was just as passionate and obsessed about the thing as I was. And our vision of the movie was exactly the same."

For a mainstream Hollywood film, *Billy Madison* cost relative peanuts; once the studio replaced Kessler with Davis and saw that filming was moving along, the Universal *machers* more or less left the filmmakers to their own devices. "There weren't any expectations other than to try to make their money back," Davis reasons, "which wasn't going to be that hard." The movie opened February 10, 1995—Presidents' Day weekend, a typically sleepy turn of the box-office cycle. In its opening weekend, it grossed $6,639,080, making *Billy Madison* the number one film in the country. The picture would go on to earn nearly $26.5 million in theaters—chump change compared to 1995's biggest comedy (the $108 million *Ace Ventura* sequel, *When Nature Calls*), but enough to keep Sandler in the game.

As expected, the reviews were dismal. The *Toronto Star*, writing of a movie shot in its backyard, pegged *Billy Madison* as "a vulgar, idiotic mess." The storied Texan alternative weekly the *Austin Chronicle*, strangely mirroring Downey's speech in the film, disparaged *Billy Madison* as "one of the most outrageously bad movies in recent memory, a misfire...ridiculously and consistently off-target from anything remotely resembling a good film." Many critics speciously lumped the movie with the "gross-out" comedies that were then in vogue or unfavorably compared Sandler to the year's big star, Jim Carrey. Peter Rainer, writing in the *Los Angeles Times*, scolded Sandler for "trying to be the King of the Peepee and Doodoo jokes," while the *San Francisco Examiner*, in a fit of melodrama, reported that "we're raising an entire generation of audience that doesn't know what good is." Siskel & Ebert, America's then-reigning face of populist film criticism, united to denounce the movie. "Am I getting older, or do I have taste?" Gene Siskel posited in *At the Movies*. "I think I have taste—*Billy Madison* is pretty lame."

"Adam Sandler has a problem," Roger Ebert echoed. "That is, he's not an attractive screen presence. He might have a future as a villain or as a fall-guy or the butt of a joke, but as the protagonist...he re-creates the fingernails-on-the-blackboard syndrome. You can't stand him!"

Of the major newspaper critics, only the *New York Times*'s Janet Maslin was less than hostile, conceding in her tepid review that the picture "succeeds as a reasonably smart no-brainer." Even in trifling critical quarters, *Billy Madison* was slaughtered. I distinctly recall editing a pan in my college paper written by a pie-faced freshman; he filed his article garbed in new khaki slacks, a massive manufacturer's sticker still affixed to the side.

Reviewing movies is no walk in the park, and comedies prove especially tough. A drama or action movie can be digested in private, but the success of humor depends on the audience. ("It sounds stupid, but the air tells you what your night is going to be like," my favorite comedian, Joan Rivers, once told me in an interview. "You can tell what the crowd's like within three minutes.") A critic screening *Billy Madison* would not be surrounded by stoned 14-year-olds, but rather by scattered colleagues—an overeducated, underpaid collection of professional cynics predisposed to grumbling, not laughter. And a critic has little to gain in praising a film like *Billy Madison*, with its ostensibly boorish jokes and unproven star. His editor will question his judgment and he will stand alone among his peers. Readers, especially older ones, will look askance. Particularly with broader comedy, what is funny on-screen can fall dead on paper, exposing a critic to that embarrassing sensation in which a person relays a beloved joke only to meet blank stares. To praise a comedian before others jump onboard—to be the first in the room to laugh—is to open oneself to vulnerability. And who needs that?

Not surprisingly, as younger critics screened the movie with fresh eyes in the years to come, its stock ballooned. I asked my friends David Fear and Joshua Rothkopf, film critics at *Time Out New York* (where I work as a music critic), to assess *Billy Madison*. "If you discovered Sandler via his later comedies, you'd just think of the guy as another frat-friendly poster-boy riding a wave of Neanderthal doofusness," Fear claims. "But Sandler's an absurdist at heart—and *Billy Madison* is the only movie where he's fully embraced that off-the-scale side of his humor. It's a truly fucked-up movie."

"Sandler's career has been so hit-and-miss for me that to see him completely owning something is a rare treat," Rothkopf counters. "I love how anarchic and infantile he allows himself to be. And yet it's never harsh, like *Punch-Drunk Love*. It's gleeful and unencumbered."

"There were all kinds of things in that movie that you see in later movies," Jim Downey reasons. "It's kind of seminal. It was unapologetically indulgent and certainly fearless. There were really brilliant things and wacky things and raunchy things. It had all of Adam's sensibility."

Nonetheless, the criticism that perhaps most echoes prevailing thought among comedy cognoscenti occurred in a 2001 episode of Judd Apatow's sitcom *Undeclared*, in which Sandler appears as himself. "*Billy Madison*, that was, like, punk rock," a character informs the star. "Everything after that…I just didn't like."

....

The year after I encountered *Billy Madison*, I spent the summer at my parents' home once more, teaching tennis to suburban children. Day after day, my co-workers and I fed balls under the blistering sun, repeating phrases like "Low to high," "Punch your volley," and "Danny, stop pretending your racket is a guitar" as if they were Buddhist mantras. I liked my fellow instructors—many of us had grown up playing tennis together—but at this point I shared little with them beyond the sport. One day, feeding balls alongside a muscular co-worker—I always imagined that he was called "The Moose" or "Tiny" by his fraternity brothers—it came out that I was an aficionado of *Billy Madison*. "Ah," he said sagely, nodding a head that for years I had assumed to be empty. "I prefer *Happy Gilmore*." Later, picking up balls, the gentle giant approached me. "I have a theory about why some people like *Billy Madison* and others *Happy Gilmore*," he disclosed.

I drew closer to my co-worker, as if he were about to slip me confidential information disproving the Warren Commission. "What is it?" I asked.

"People who drink beer like *Happy Gilmore*," he posited. "People who smoke pot like *Billy Madison*."

"Oh," I said.

Parsing my co-worker's words, I think he was implying that

Billy Madison is a surreal work, cerebral and uncanny, whereas Sandler's next movie was by comparison blunt and aggressive. Directed by Dennis Dugan from another script by Sandler and Herlihy (with uncredited additions by Apatow), *Happy Gilmore* came out in 1996, the year after *Billy Madison*. It is a golf comedy made in the wake of *Caddyshack*, which seems akin to writing a tragedy about a troubled Danish prince after *Hamlet*. Sandler partisans tend to link *Happy Gilmore* with *Billy Madison*. "To me, *Billy Madison* and *Happy Gilmore* are sort of like the early Marx Brothers movies," Jim Downey says. "The stuff Adam did later can be more like later Marx Brothers movies, when they got less crazy and random and their movies became more about story."

Yet despite winning the beery approbation of my big-hitting colleague, *Happy Gilmore* is inferior to its predecessor. In many ways, the sports film sets the stage for Sandler's subsequent work. Its jokes are easier. Actors play against type (an ass-kicking Bob Barker) and send up past performances (Carl Weathers as a golf pro). Product placement runs rampant, nullifying any of the innocence and anarchy from the previous film. Many jokes involve Sandler berating or striking people—not children, sadly, but adults. Notwithstanding a nicely cruel Ben Stiller cameo, the side characters are largely rote, lacking the whimsicality of, say, *Billy Madison*'s black mammy maid. Moreover, unlike the previous film, *Happy Gilmore* can seem sloppy and cheap. It is funny yet pedestrian—the laughs remain, but the magic is gone.

After the charmed experience with *Billy Madison*, Sandler had approached Davis about directing *Happy Gilmore*. "I just felt like I needed to do something else as a director," she explains. "I can't say I regret not doing it, because I think [*Happy Gilmore*] is great. But in a sense, I do feel sad that I'm not part of that group anymore."

Dugan, who prior to *Happy Gilmore* had directed *Problem Child* and the *Night at the Opera* tribute *Brain Donors*, went on to helm a number of Sandler projects. Some of these films are lousy (1999's *Big Daddy*) and others deeply flawed (2006's *I Now Pronounce You Chuck and Larry*). But one is outstanding: 2008's *You Don't Mess with the Zohan,* which stars Sandler as a randy Mossad agent unleashed in New York. After *Billy Madison, The Zohan* marks the brightest moment in the actor's spotty filmography.

Sandler's career is atypical. As he became an unlikely Hollywood goliath, the comedian surrounded himself with a posse of nearly-ran comedians, former *SNL* cast members and seemingly every other person who was kind to him during the sliver of adulthood before he became famous. He shuns the press. Print interviews are verboten (even to publications as

Adam Sandler's Career in Pictograms

Illustration by Phillip Niemeyer

eminent as the *Lowbrow Reader*), a ban that has cast Sandler in a veil of inscrutability. According to the office of his manager, Sandy Wernick, this silence extends to associates such as Herlihy, who work closely with Sandler's production company, Happy Madison.

Affectionately named for those first two films, Happy Madison movies share an aesthetic with *Billy Madison*, catering to boys suffering through the indignities of early puberty. They are refreshingly unpretentious. Too often, however, the movies fall prey to the clichés that his debut sent up. Sandler is known to take flops badly; perhaps as a result, his pictures can be frustratingly safe. When he strays from his comfort zone— as in Paul Thomas Anderson's *Punch-Drunk Love* or Apatow's *Funny People*—the results are intriguing, but he quickly retreats to known territory. Aiming for the middle, Sandler maintains a secure career for himself and his tent of dependents while ignoring his artistic legacy. The bulk of his work remains altogether appealing and critically underrated. Yet it is beneath him.

Regardless, it is with a steadfast loyalty that I have not shown to many of my own relatives that I have stuck by the star as fan. In 1998, on one of our first dates, I took my girlfriend to see *The Waterboy*, along with two carloads of my friends. ("I still don't know what you were thinking," she says now.) I reviewed Sandler's maudlin *Click* for a magazine, but could not find it in my heart to pan it. I began publishing the *Lowbrow Reader*, initially as a response to *Billy Madison*'s critical reception. And in 2010, as Sandler was promoting *Grown Ups*—an ensemble film co-starring Rock, Spade and others—I went to the Ed Sullivan Theater to watch him tape a spot on *The Late Show with David Letterman*. (Events had conspired against my having a working television, so it seemed like the only surefire way to catch the appearance.) *Late Show* studio tapings are notoriously disappointing. Many people recoil upon seeing the showbiz apparatus revealed with workmanlike cynicism, but I find a kinship with my own fast-fading vocation, journalism. Letterman—Krusty the Clown himself—stands aloof from guests and audience. He resembles a comfortable human being on the monitor and an ungainly fake person in the flesh. He blasts air conditioning, to keep the room on its toes, and Paul Shaffer's music, so that he does not have to speak to anybody during breaks. Before the cameras rolled, as Sandler waited in the wings, Letterman gave his guest a cursory wave. Sandler generally excels on the talk-

Adam Sandler in Punch-Drunk Love / Illustration by Doreen Kirchner

show couch, but this day he seemed slightly off his game, even missing a cue from the famously quick host. Like many people years into a difficult job, the star seemed weary. "People always [say], 'That must have been the best time ever, a lot of practical jokes,'" Sandler told Letterman about working with his old cronies in *Grown Ups*. "Comedians don't do that. Comedians are, like, very angry all the time."

My deeper Sandler pilgrimage had occurred a decade earlier, in 2000. By then, I had moved to Manhattan; my brother had enrolled in college in Massachusetts. It was the first time we were living within driving distance of each other in many years. When Sandler's *Little Nicky* came out, I boarded a Greyhound bus to Boston so that I could see the film with my brother. My girlfriend dropped me off at Port Authority, like a soldier going off to war. "You are a moron," the pitying look in her eyes told me. But I was excited to see my younger sibling; I had long fantasized about drawing closer to him as he grew into adulthood.

My brother picked me up at Boston's bus depot and we drove to a theater on the edge of town. Not long after the movie started, his cell phone rang; to my horror, he answered it. "Yeah, I'm at this movie with my brother," he said casually. When his phone rang a second time, I glared at him; he rolled his eyes and took the call in the lobby, returning to the theater 20 minutes later. When the picture ended he sprang from his seat, as if dismissed from detention. "So what did you think?" I asked.

"Sucked," he mumbled.

"Well, *I* thought it was funny," I said. "It kind of has the same theme as *Billy Madison*, even if it's obviously not as good. And Rodney Dangerfield's in it!"

"Whatever," my brother said. As we drove on, I increasingly got the sense that he would rather be spending time with people who were not me. Anybody would do: his new college friends, a hobo, our Uncle Sol. I returned to New York demoralized; nothing is more embarrassing than unmatched enthusiasm.

As it so happened, *Little Nicky* would mark a turning point for Sandler. With the film, he launched Happy Madison while concluding his working relationship with Simonds, the producer. It would be the actor's final writing collaboration with Herlihy and, with the exception of 2008's aberrant *Zohan*, his last flat-out screwball film. Soon, his characters would be given wives, children and jobs. His cinematic adolescence had ended.

"Around the time of *Little Nicky*, I met with Adam and Herlihy to talk about working together again," Tamra Davis says. "Herlihy was like, 'You know, Adam's different than the guy we worked with back then. He's grown up.' In a sense, Herlihy and I have a great memory of that time. And I'm sure that Adam does, too. I don't know if we could ever re-create it—that freshness, that ability to just be free and have fun."

Of course, Sandler grew up. Just as my brother could not spend life as a 14-year-old innocent, lurking in a pot-fogged Eden, and, after a few shoves, I relented to adulthood myself. Is this not the central theme of *Billy Madison*? Amid all the madness, Billy ultimately meets his fate, forsaking a life of whimsy intent on the responsibilities and tedium of adulthood. It traps the best of us. Yet every time I revisit *Billy Madison*—my favorite movie, my brother's favorite movie and I suspect Adam Sandler's favorite movie—I am taken back to that long-ago summer, when the clouds suddenly parted and I tumbled into the rabbit hole created by Sandler, Davis and the rest in this majestically berserk film. Shame we can't all stay there.

Lowbrow Reader #8, 2010

INTERVIEW IN BERLIN

by Lee Hazlewood

MAN ENTERS DOUBLE door left. Drops several packages on floor. Takes small, very cheap tape machine from coat pocket. Turns machine on—pushes it as close as possible to my face and, finally, speaks.

"Sorry I'm late, Lee. But my wife was going to interview you and she changed her mind. I think she was frightened."

"It might be nice if you introduced yourself."

"Oh, I'm Hans." He tosses his wife's card at the tape machine.

"Okay, Hans. It's 5:45. Your wife was due here at 5:30. She was to be my last interview of the day, number 14. After 10 or 12, I get rather homicidal, particularly when I'm asked non-musical questions. So, Hans, what do you want to know about my CD?"

"First I need to know something about your family."

"Just music questions, Hans."

"Now, you have three children and—"

I get up from my desk, grab Hans by the nape of his neck and walk him to the nearest window. "Look down—four floors—and get your shit together. Or out you go, Hans. We're about to discover if scribes and reindeer really know how to fly."

"I don't believe Anna would approve."

"I suppose Anna is your wife."

Hans shakes his head "Yes."

Illustration by Nathan Gelgud

"Well, I don't give a fuck, Hans. You go now—out that door, or out this window."

Hans quickly gathers his packages and tape machine and hops briskly to the door. Two PR people from the record company enter the room. "Any problems, Lee?" they ask in unison.

"My problem just ran out that door."

"He did seem in a hurry." One of the PR persons pours a scotch and I sit down on the couch. As the cool scotch touches my lips, the double doors open and the head of Hans appears.

"Lee, would you have time to sign a few of these old albums for my wife's friends?"

"Call the police and an ambulance. I'm throwing him out the—"

Hans's head disappears and the sound of running footsteps is heard...by all...on the fourth floor...of a Berlin hotel...on a day in May...2002.

Lowbrow Reader #3, 2003

CARTOON HOUR
by David Berman

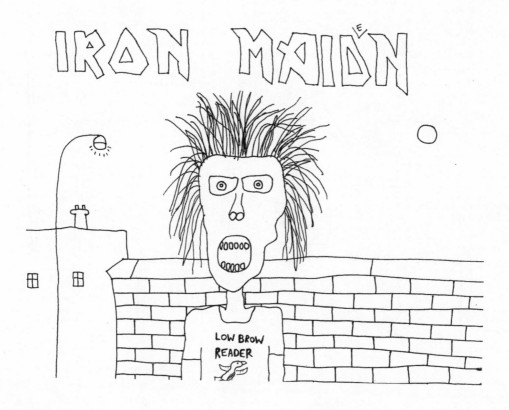

PUEBLO, COLORADO

BRICKTEARDROP

FOR BRITPOP.

xmas tree tetris

ARBOR DAY

Lowbrow Reader #7 (2009) & #8 (2010)

JOAN RIVERS:
A BITCH IN NEW YORK

by Jay Ruttenberg

F OR YEARS, THE most engaging and outrageous stand-up
comic in New York City has not been some downtown
wunderkind, pie-faced and aloof, but rather a shrill old woman
with a famously plasticized visage and the moral compass of a
third-world dictator. I write, of course, about the fabulous Joan
Rivers who, in the twilight of a remarkably durable career—in
the course of a single set, she might refer to herself as being 70,
75 and then 73 years old—has struck an unlikely and in many
ways unprecedented creative stride.

Rivers is increasingly known best for her role grilling
celebrities at the red-carpet arrivals of award shows, alongside
her daughter, Melissa. She also sells tacky jewelry via the
Internet. But it is as a stand-up that Rivers emits the unmistakable
glow of a world-class performer; this is particularly so when
she has a suitable audience. Until the club was shuttered this
March, her favored home base of the last few years was Fez
Under Time Café, a snug cabaret space situated in the basement
of a Moroccan restaurant downtown. I observed a number of
these performances, including a series during the club's final
month.

At Fez—or "this dump, Fez," as the comedian lovingly tagged
it—Rivers's audience was split roughly evenly between Long
Island yentas and Chelsea homosexuals. It is difficult to imagine

two groups more compatible with Rivers. Both are catty, brash, obnoxiously loud and eager to mock themselves. Most critically, each demographic, at least on the surface, demonstrates that rare gift to such a comedian: utter ethical bankruptcy. The comedian seized this offering with the appreciation of a freshly released inmate biting into his welcome-home dinner.

While Rivers's set differed from show to show, she would return habitually to a series of topics. One was Michael Jackson: "Millions of dollars for one night with Michael Jackson?"[1] she would say. "*Achhh!* If only I had a son, I'd send him straight to

---

[1] Miss Rivers's phrasing changed from week to week; I have stuck to her exact words as much as possible, but many of the quotations here are paraphrased.

Illustration by Tom Sanford

Neverland." Here, her voice would assume the hectoring tone of a mother forcing her child to visit a relative: "You bend over and do this for mommy!"

Perhaps her funniest joke revolves around Melissa, who, Rivers would inform the audience, was offered $500,000 to pose for *Playboy* but turned the magazine down. "The nerve of that bitch!" Rivers roared. "She's been divorced for three years and I'm still paying off her wedding. I'm 75 fucking years old, standing on a red carpet saying, *Who are you wearing? Who are you?* $500,000, and she turns it down?!? Pull down your pants and show them the pussy!"

Week in, week out, however, the touchiest subject would be the comedian's evocation of September 11th. As soon as Rivers said the words "World Trade," the yentas would begin a knee-jerk hiss—a sound clearly relished by the performer, who has a rotating stable of jokes about the tragedy. In one, she wonders: "If you knew what was going to happen on September 11th—who would you invite to breakfast at the World Trade Center? *Eggs Benedict...Windows on the World...It'll be our make-up brunch!*" Her more common punch line revolved around 9/11 widows, a group she deemed among the most fortunate in New York. "What would you rather have?" she inquired. "Six million dollars—or a man lying next to you in bed farting, with a big fat stomach and his balls lying out?"

Other topics might include Lizzie Grubman ("a blonde angel who wants to rid the Hamptons of white trash"); Helen Keller and Anne Frank (both disparaged as "whiners"); Rosie O'Donnell (whom she impersonates coming out of the closet by squatting into a Neanderthal pose, thrusting a bony finger at the audience and mannishly grunting, "I got a surprise for you"); and whoever was sitting in front of the stage (one young woman was informed that her engagement ring was acceptable for goyim, but "swimming jewelry" for a Jew).

Mostly, the gays would swallow it all with expected irony—after all, a drag act like Kiki and Herb can be nearly as nasty—while the Long Island women would nod their frizzy heads in accord. What's fuzzy is where Rivers herself stands. The comedian has given herself an outer shell of exaggerated wickedness: Her notorious appetite for plastic surgery has lent her face a permanent air of diva pride and disdain. She celebrates stealing, avarice and wearing fur. She insists that only a fool would marry for love. ("You want an orgasm?" she says. "Marry a rich old troll and wait for him to say, 'Do you want mink or sable?'") During her performances, she professed a hatred for the Chinese, American Indians, old people, fat people, poor people, blind people, the Olsen twins and a man in the audience who said he didn't watch her at the Oscars. And while Rivers claims not to have voted in the last presidential election—based on the science that both candidates had ugly daughters—she says she became a Republican when Amy Carter wore glasses at her own wedding.

Yet one remains suspect of this wonderful comedian's dubious integrity. Proceeds from her weekly set at Fez, where she unleashed her vitriol for over three years, were donated to two charities: Guide Dogs for the Blind and God's Love We Deliver, a service that brings meals to AIDS patients. Naturally, Rivers vented about the recipients of both charities: No blind person ever poked her with a cane and said "thank you," while, because of advances in medicine, the AIDS patients she was helping were refusing to die. ("I've been delivering dinner to the same fucking asshole for three years," Rivers would cry. "And he's getting *fat!*")

It should be noted that this woman, so eager to denounce sentiment and weakness, lost her husband to suicide in the '80s. Naturally, she has a whole catalog of jokes about her tragedy. How could she not?! Put into this context, the foul-mouthed widow may remind many of another famous brat: the great Courtney Love. Both performers are shrewd, spiteful blondes, plastic and proud, with the astuteness to recognize the word "bitch" as a compliment. Each has a captivating stage presence, teetering between domineering control and rambling chaos.

Once, during her Fez show, an audience member asked Rivers about Courtney Love. (This was soon after the rock star's week of infamy in New York, when she exposed herself both to David Letterman and to diners at a local Wendy's.) The comedian praised the singer for killing her husband and getting away with it, then declared Love's situation "very sad." It is tempting to revisit an old cliché about crying comedians. It is that much more alluring, however, to hope that Rivers was speaking with customary irony.

Lowbrow Reader #5, 2006

MY TV DON'T WORK NO MORE: A TRIBUTE TO *WINGS*

by Neil Michael Hagerty

IT'S BEEN A rough year for me, I don't mind telling you. I wish I had eyeglasses an inch thick but they don't make them anymore. Everything tends to the streamlined now. Even the most lascivious or obese fellow might appear stylish and in the game. All year, all these women have been trying to skin me, so I had to take a few months of respite on the couch. And when I'm on the couch, I watch TV.

Most television these days is made for the all-important busy and productive viewer. Niche tastes have proliferated to such an extent that channel surfing has become a laborious task that requires attentive research. Viewing choices have narrowed from a plural vision of the entirety into a fragmented babel of direct marketing. Every choice is focused in a sliver-slim two-way peephole baring but a single element of the whole. In the past, the formally limited three-network valve filtered all efforts directed into the clutch of televised media and revealed so much more detail in a simplistic and highly refined monument of explicative images. A vast resource of useful information was hidden within the multicolored video bands, revealed in abstract and cold solidity each night after Carson and the National Anthem closed out the programming day. A sustained wail blared infernally along with the test pattern of rectangular stripes and ushered in the timeless period of meditation when the all-seeing eye rolled back into its head to re-energize by scanning the dreams of America. A sense of widespread reality could be divined from within this grotesque public sorcery. The Titans have since discovered that we are more than willing to design smaller aisles of content for them. They need only to control one of the tributaries of the big river. You call it choice; I call it "a cop on every corner."

It was hard to fall into a groove, there on the couch. I had to keep checking the schedule and flipping around to piece together a semblance of the programming day. It was late at night when I started to watch reruns of *Wings*, the sitcom that aired from 1990 to 1997. I have now watched the entire run, and I believe that *Wings* represents a critical bridge from the past television paradigm. *Wings* addresses much of the confusion and sickening vulnerability that ushered in the abuses of our current "on-demand" system. It also demonstrates a crucial lesson about struggling to make clear choices in a world where selfish and sensation-absorbed insularity is encouraged.

The series begins with a premise: Two brothers are reunited after their father's death because his will forces them to do so. Joe (played by Tim Daly) is an orderly hometown boy running a small commuter airline in Nantucket. His younger brother Brian (Steven Weber) is a feckless and irresponsible layabout who ran off with Joe's wife years before and has been drifting around the Bahamas. They are both pilots. It comes about that Brian has been dumped by Joe's ex-wife and, upon returning home, is invited to stay and fly planes for Joe's airline, Sandpiper Air. Initially, the two brothers compete for the affections of Helen Chappel (Crystal Bernard), a formerly obese childhood friend who is now beautiful. She runs the lunch counter in the small Tom Nevers airfield, where most of the action of *Wings* takes place. Helen speaks in a thick Southern accent, which is explained away in passing—something to do with moving back to Texas for a time. She plays the cello and dreams, off and on, of leaving for greater career opportunities.

Eventually, Joe and Helen begin a relationship that breaks apart and resolves over the course of the series. This leads to the introduction of two female characters as foils to Brian. Alex (Farrah Forke) is a strong-willed and glamorous helicopter pilot. She departs and is replaced by Helen's prissy and demanding sister Casey (the brilliant Amy Yasbeck), who returns to the island after being dumped by her husband. There is a stable ensemble of town denizens, including the grotesque Roy, a dumb mechanic, an old woman and an Italian cabdriver.

But the premise was diminished soon into the series's run, as theatrical conventions such as dramatic polysemy, bathos and farce provided the main content of *Wings*. By building the show on this foundation, *Wings* never put its faith or hope for survival in the potential of its characters or premise. Rather, *Wings* changed dynamics and destroyed its own credibility with each passing episode. It responded to trends and styles. Since it was built on the classical fundamentals of comedy merely adorned by the conventions of the sitcom, the wavering attractiveness of the lead characters and the disposability of their goals never hurt the potential for comedy to damage their lives without remission. *Wings* accumulated comic situations but not the restraints imposed by the management of a consistent tone. For example, *Seinfeld* always had to maintain a certain formulaic distance from the conventions of a premise-based show such as *I Dream of Jeannie* and could never resort to dramatic character interaction.

Wings, however, could flirt with whatever tone would lend itself to satisfying humor, whether it

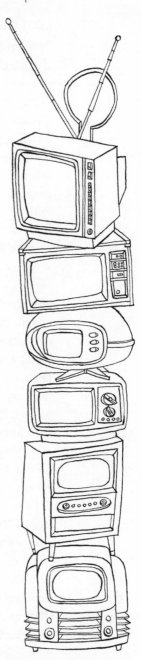

Illustration by Carson Ellis

meant posing dramatic choices that grew out of character development or rationing out jokes to the characters as types within the predictable limitations of a weekly sitcom. Unlike realistic sitcoms such as *Roseanne* or *The Cosby Show*, it was possible for *Wings* to explode the boundaries of premise temporarily without having to rationally explain the alteration. The characters on *Wings* often mention past events, but no matter how severe the comedic damage might be, it is absorbed back into the characters as they fight always to return to the banality they claim to despise. When Roseanne won the lottery, this exploding of the entire framework of her show diminished its strength by removing the limitations of the characters, who were merely revealed to be the same people—only with money. I enjoyed the brave self-destruction of this show, but the implosion was never complete. And it paled in comparison to the writing and ensemble acting of the early seasons that depicted such minute struggles and terrors as "Dan and Roseanne can't find time to have sex" or "Jackie slept with Arnie." The early character-driven comedy could even allow for dramatic episodes, like one in which Dan beats up Jackie's abusive boyfriend. The events always resolved back into the characters, but had to be carried forward as they grew because they were "real." When the family won the lottery, the characters grew at a realistic rate and the show resisted the absurdity imposed upon it. Because *Wings* consistently undermined and even attempted to destroy its characters, such sad events as infidelity, house fires, mental illness, death and plane crashes were handled on both a realistic level (within the limited, selfish natures of the characters) and on an absurd level (by exploiting any possibility for a cheap joke).

The popular reality and acceptance of the characters derived from the theatrical technique of the actors. Because the characters were types alternately struggling against and embracing their mundanity, *Wings* used broad theatricality to communicate the characters' inner lives. Expansive and optimistic behavior was consistently met with crushing defeat. Watching the characters struggle under the oppression of this justice makes their fates both sympathetic and satisfying. The characters are always actors and never hope to simulate a family of ciphers that we must take into our hearts. *Wings* never valued its characters over a joke. This can be a killing flaw in most sitcoms, as the characters must possess some sort of iconic power to keep the show alive long after the formula becomes tired. *Wings*, however, started out tired, stayed tired and prospered.

As with many sitcoms, much of the strength came through the side characters. Thomas Haden Church played Lowell, the mechanic. In his exaggerated garb of jumpsuit, tool belt and cap he was the Urkel, or Rerun, of *Wings*. Lowell provided non sequitur responses, slapstick physical japes and "stupid" misreadings of reality. Rebecca Schull played Fay, the aged attendant at the Sandpiper Air counter. She was an ex-stewardess from the golden days who had widowed three husbands, all named George. With her pleasing matronly ways, she provided opportunity for situations based on age stereotypes and jokes in the form of inappropriately devilish comments that contradicted her appearance. Tony Shalhoub, an American of Lebanese descent, played the doomed Italian cabdriver Antonio in the broadest possible accent. Shalhoub has not been typecast or trapped forever in this role (unlike Costanza or Cliff the Postman) both because of this simple distancing device and the cumulative effect of the repellent aspects of the show as a whole. Whereas "Costanza" is a tour-de-force performance that created an inescapably iconic identity for the actor Jason Alexander, "Antonio" is a tour de force of acting that distanced Tony Shalhoub from the character by distancing the character from the audience.

Television is a wasteland of unintended consequences, and love flows to the most unlikely flaws within the attractive whole, creating in memory a monument devoid of details. If a show becomes popular to the point of defining its viewers' identities, all action within the structure is unfailing until it loses its audience. *Wings* avoided this burden throughout its run. Although nothing makes sense like success, it remains to be judged if such unflagging identification has egregious effects. Allegorically, the process seems destructive, and Tony Shalhoub's characterization (and *Wings* as a whole) suggests a method of challenging predetermination, fate and oblivion.

Wings is a compendium of such circular allegory, a closed network that contains and accidentally reveals stunning details through its efforts to retain a successful structure. It reduces the old form of television as an entity into one show. Sadly, it is a Ouija board that speaks only of the past. When I had completed the course of the show I was able to lift myself off the couch and overcome the deliberation that had been afflicting me. The debilitation I had imagined was replaced by a method of perception both artificial yet efficacious; a simulacra that imitated the process that *Wings* applied to the inherent reflexivity of television. When a show (or an entire network) focuses narrowly on a single subject such as the houses of celebrities or the remodeling of an old motorcycle, the negation of the tighter structure precludes any helpful revelations, which can only come when a presiding body attempts to read the common mind. The narrow focus shields a controlling entity from revealing more than desired. There can never be a *Wings* network, but if competition in the cable and broadcast industry is ever wisely reformed, the utilitarian potential of television could be restored. Our current plight can be viewed as a transitional phase—a phase that *Wings* both predicted and reflected but never presumed to resolve.

Lowbrow Reader #4, 2004

LETTER FROM THE EDITOR: LOST YOUTH

by Jay Ruttenberg

W HEN WAS IT that I got so mature and started washing my hands after using the bathroom? When did I stop waking up in the middle of the night, sticking a sausage inside a Drake's Devil Dog and calling it "supper"? When did I stop shipping my socks and underwear from New York to Florida so that my mother could launder and fold them in that special way of hers, returning them with notes of confidence to prepare me for an arduous workweek of seeing patients in court?

Why, it seems like only yesterday that I had all my hair, both on my head and stuffed in my pillow in lieu of fancy cottons. It seems like just days ago that I was running wild at grade-school recess, playing hopscotch and double-Dutch jump rope. "Get away from the children!" the teacher would say. But we would keep on jumping rope until they'd drag me away, chanting about Cinderella being dressed in yella all the way to the holding pen, where the drunks and I would laugh and laugh till the wee hours of the night, at which point they would beat me senseless.

Michael Jackson! Remember when that name conjured up images of a singing sensation, not a man threatening to sue you if you keep sneaking onto his property and using his *Pirates of the Caribbean* ride? Remember a time when he said things like, "Billie Jean is not my lover" and not, "Sir, you are clearly not an underage cancer patient and the Make-a-Wish foundation didn't send you to my house—now get your hand out of my pants or I'm calling security."

Oh, lost youth! How I would crank up the Doobie Brothers, light incense candles and have the nurse tell patients I was running late, while in truth I was in the examining room, masturbating. Could it really be so long ago that I was at Yankee Stadium, wrestling a game-winning ball from an impish youngster with such rambunctious force that he broke his wrist? Was it really a lifetime ago that I sold the ball on eBay and used the money to hire the great surgeon Patrick D. Bradt to autograph the boy's cast?

What has happened to our golden days, when my generation took to the streets demanding a more lucrative contract for Howard Stern? When did we start voting for Republicans and Democrats rather than writing in the names of *Caddyshack* characters? When did we start sleeping in houses of our own rather than squatting in those of CEOs whom we'd lure away to a Jamaican resort by saying they'd won a month-long vacation as a reward for all their great purchases, knowing full-well that they'd be too proud not to just pay the bill, and by that point we'd have stolen all their family photos, anyway?

To any young person who reads this now, I implore you: Do not wake up one day and find yourself all grown up and full of regrets for not having had that affair with your brother's wife or discovering what it feels like to sell crack to poor people. If you've been waiting to tell your grandmother that she's a crotchety old hag, just remember—someday, she won't be around to hear you! Do not miss your chance to spend April Fools' Day telling patient after patient that they only have a week to live, excepting the one patient who truly is dying, whom you inform has only an hour left before regaling him with a 45-minute story about your golf game. Do not end up like me: A rueful man, staring down his golden years; alone but for his wife, mistress and mistress's unusually sympathetic husband; crying himself to sleep at night knowing that he has never been elected to the United States Senate or pictured on the local news leaping over a puddle the day of a nasty storm.

Lowbrow Reader #6, 2008

Illustration by John Mathias

HIDDEN CITIZEN

Rediscovering the Brilliant,
Funny Novels of Gilbert Rogin

by Jay Jennings

R EVIEWING GILBERT ROGIN'S novel *What Happens Next?* in
Partisan Review in 1973, Joyce Carol Oates wrote, "Because
Rogin is...very funny his work is in danger of being underestimated...." To make a Roginesque joke, his work has been so
widely underestimated, it might take a metaphysician to prove its
existence. Each of his three books—a collection of stories, *The
Fencing Master* (1965); and two novels assembled mostly from
published stories, *What Happens Next?* (1971) and *Preparations
for the Ascent* (1980)—went out of print in short order. His deac-
cessioning from the public libraries of America has proceeded
apace, so that many of the copies available on used-book aggre-
gator Bookfinder.com are "ex-library." Nor are any extant in the
New York Public Library's circulating branches—in his native
city where his work is set! A lonely one copy of each turned
up in the NYPL's noncirculating CATNYP database, along
with the plaintive software query to my "Gilbert Rogin" search,
"Do you mean 'gilbert groin'?" (I think Rogin would appreciate
that anagrammatical query, since he both anatomizes libidinal
adventures and plays inventively with language.)

Of course, most writers suffer the fate of obscurity, but
most have not had such an enviable literary career. Between
1963 and 1980, Rogin published 33 stories in the *New Yorker*
and others in *Esquire*, *Harper's* and *Vogue*; he won an Academy

Award for literature from the American Academy of Arts and Letters (in 1972, along with Harry Crews, Paula Fox and Thomas McGuane); and his novels have received high, sometimes rapturous, praise in reviews. Besides Oates's lauding of his "unique vision" in *What Happens Next?*, Anatole Broyard, the *New York Times*'s primary reviewer, found the book's "sardonic dialogue" superior to Donald Barthelme's and its portrait of marriage on a par with John Updike's Maple stories. Poet and critic L.E. Sissman, writing in the *New York Times Book Review*, declared at the outset of his review, "I think Gilbert Rogin has written a great novel, the first one I've run across in quite some time." Nine years later, his next and last book, *Preparations for the Ascent*, received less attention, but Mordecai Richler, admitting in the *Times Book Review* that he was not familiar with Rogin's work, found it "subtle, original, and refreshingly intelligent." And in his 1979 introduction to Polish novelist Bruno Schulz's *Sanatorium under the Sign of the Hourglass*, Updike himself—after comparing Schulz to Kafka and Proust—invoked one of Rogin's *New Yorker* stories, linking the two as "writers in a world of hidden citizens" who "work with an excited precision, pulling silver threads from the coarse texture of daily life."

It was in that canonized company that, recently happening upon Updike's essay in his collection *Hugging the Shore*, I first heard of Rogin's fiction. His name, however, I knew well. When I started working as a reporter at *Sports Illustrated* in 1987, Rogin had recently departed as managing editor, the magazine's top post, after a 30-year career there, and his name still echoed in the halls. He then moved to the science magazine *Discover* and later to a lofty Time Inc. corporate editorial position, from which he retired in 1992. (Among other accomplishments, he helped Quincy Jones found *Vibe*.) Updike's anointing sent me to my *Complete New Yorker* DVD, where I found Rogin's stories, before later seeking out his books from the above-mentioned used-book site.

The questions that pricked me amid the amassed encomiums were "How does such a lauded writer disappear so thoroughly?" and "Is he really worthy of resurrection?" Or, to put it in another anagram of his name, "Lit gig reborn?" I wondered if Rogin, born in 1929, might be a male analogue to Paula Fox, six years his elder, whose out-of-print oeuvre in adult fiction had been revived by a Jonathan Franzen essay declaring her

Illustration by Doreen Kirchner

novel *Desperate Characters* to be "obviously superior to any novel by Fox's contemporaries John Updike, Philip Roth and Saul Bellow." I doubt I'd venture that far into hyperbole, but could Rogin, like Fox a chronicler of New York City angst, have been unfairly overshadowed by better-known peers?

I worked backward from the most recent book, ending with the short stories, which, while skillfully rendered, seemed to be a warm-up for the two novels. Those books essentially comprise one long narrative of a marriage and its entropic dissolution; Julian and Daisy in *What Happens Next?* become Albert and the similarly floral Violet in *Preparations for the Ascent,* and the later book largely picks up in chronology where the other one ends. (Strangely, in the latter, Rogin doesn't change the name of the wife's wastrel ex, Skippy Mountjoy, or those of the family dachshunds, Josh and Jake.) The protagonist, no matter the name, is a (presumably autobiographical) middle-aged, Jewish, Manhattanite male, a magazine writer of eclectic intellectual interests and eccentric habits. If Stendhal defined the novel as a "mirror being carried down a highway," Rogin's carrier stares at himself in the mirror while lugging it up West End Avenue to his therapist's office or to Madison Square Garden for a basketball game. He moves from place to place in accord with his daily duties as husband and son, lover and friend (and only rarely as employee), hilariously hyperobservant of the world around him while pondering his "immobilized," abstracted personality ("the Apollonian and Dionysian sides of character being of equal strength"). "The trouble with you, Julian," his wife tells him in *What Happens Next?,* "is that you have no outer life."

Rogin's dialogue is often slightly stylized, which heightens the humor. In *Preparations for the Ascent,* Albert, separated from his wife, moves mere blocks away and can see her building from his.

"Oh, God," his mom had said when Albert told her where he had moved. "You can hear her hair dryer from there. Couldn't you have put more ground between yourselves?"

"It wasn't premeditated," Albert said. "It was a supervenient turn of events. If you visualize the marriage as a ship that has broken up, you will see us as two shipmates clinging to opposite ends of a large piece of flotsam."

"I see you as two idiots awash on a delusion," his dad said.

There are echoes of Woody Allen in both the heady nature of the jokes and the slapstick of what little action actually does occur. He bangs heads with his dachshund; he extricates his stepson from the locked bathroom by delivering "a well-aimed kick at the doorknob, remembering—ah! too late—that he is barefoot"; he demonstrates to his wife the most efficient route to answer the telephone in the living room from the bedroom—"if you take the first turn a little wide, you'll be able to negotiate the second without decelerating. Please observe."

But there's much more than jokes and pratfalls going on here, as we are reminded on almost every page by the fineness of observation. His descriptions can be beautifully lyric (a New York sky that's blue "like the air in which Giotto's lamenting angels hover"); slyly critical (a Southern California hotel room so "grandiose" it looked "as though it had been built and furnished with an eye to the future, for the race of giants we would become"); and poignantly tactile (he remarks of his dachshund Josh, linking him with his stepson, Barney, and wondering if he's neglected them both, in an efficient, lovely elision: "How old and scruffy he is, like Barney's football, which had been kicked around the P.S. 41 schoolyard for years.")

Pinpointing why an author fails to find his audience is largely speculation, but perhaps Rogin's problem was timing. He was writing at the very apex of the market for protagonists who were middle-aged, Jewish, Manhattanite male intellectuals/writers and musers. The urtext in this genre is Saul Bellow's

Herzog (1964), with cohorts Mailer, Malamud and others doing variations on the theme. In October 1971, the same month *What Happens Next?* appeared, the influential critic Morris Dickstein identified "many years of imitation and, finally, glut in Jewish writing," and Dwight Macdonald, in November of that same year, declared *Portnoy's Complaint* (1969) "the Jewish novel to end all Jewish novels (which it unfortunately hasn't)." Even as WASPy a writer as John Updike satirized the genre and its practitioners in *Bech: A Book* in 1970, which appeared on the National Book Awards shortlist with Bellow's *Mr. Sammler's Planet*. In 1980, *Preparations for the Ascent* had the bad luck to enter a cultural world which had just the year before feted the works of similar, better established writers in his same vein: Malamud's *Dubin's Lives* and its inventively musing libidinal biographer, Roth's *The Ghost Writer* and its fantasizing historical revisionist Nathan Zuckerman, and even Woody Allen's *Manhattan*. A cursory glance at Rogin could have convinced us that we'd heard it all before.

What unifies Rogin's novels is voice and humor, but some critics of the day were flummoxed by his "inaction" heroes and the lack of a traditional plot or character development. A reviewer in Philip Rahv's journal *Modern Occasions* griped about *What Happens Next?*, "Mr. Rogin seems...resigned to recording the nonevents in Singer's life." In *New York* magazine's review of *Preparations*, novelist Evan Connell wrote, "[From Albert's] behavior you can hardly tell where he is or what he is doing. Nothing changes." Even Richler admits about *Preparations*, "...though I both enjoyed and admired it, and even laughed out loud more than once, I'm not sure I understood it" before asserting, "I'd rather be baffled by Gilbert Rogin than read a story made plain by many a more accessible but predictable writer."

Read today, Rogin's books seem fresh, the author possessed of a turn-of-the-21st-century comic sensibility more than a fundamentally Jewish one similar to his peers from the 1960s and

1970s. Obsession, and particularly self-mocking self-obsession, rather than neuroses per se are what characterize his protagonists. The criticisms above—that Rogin is merely recording nonevents or that nothing changes in his books—are identical to descriptions of *Seinfeld.* And it's no stretch to imagine *Seinfeld* mastermind Larry David in his current show, *Curb Your Enthusiasm*, holding, as Albert does, an "operative number" of 32, by which he finds "patterns" in his life, to the point that he performs actions in its multiples—sit-ups, pages read, even executing 128 strokes while making love to his girlfriend ("'I can see you moving your lips,' she says midway").

Furthermore, Rogin's experiments with narrative and self-reflexive techniques anticipate strategies adopted by the contemporary literary generation. The late David Foster Wallace's fondness for footnotes finds an ancestor in one chapter of *What Happens Next?*, when Julian uses them to record his parents' reactions to the story he's written about them. The result is a Russian doll of a read, in which he unpacks age-old parent-child anxieties while questioning narrative reliability, almost sentence by sentence. A later chapter relates an argument between Singer and Mountjoy almost entirely in police-report diction ("Singer inquired of Mountjoy who the hell he thought Singer was"), studded with excerpts from their grade-school comment cards. Other chapters feature diagrams (lunch-table accouterments as chess pieces), mathematical formulae (calculating the point C at which his and his psychiatrist's sightlines would meet), *Heartbreaking Genius*–like references to the book itself ("Regard it here in eleven-point Baskerville"), and numbered lists ("The bad things that happened on their vacation…"). Rogin's work, it seems to me, deserves that most clichéd of compliments: ahead of its time.

More evidence resides in the first pages of *What Happens Next?*, from a story originally published in 1966, in which one of Singer's TV-producing cronies envisions a game show in which a celebrity panel has to guess the problem a contestant faces ("I'm in love with a woman, but I think she's after my money") then "give the contestant two, three minutes personalized advice and comfort." The producer says, "We're liable to come up with television's lowest ebb." Perhaps not even Rogin could have envisioned *Big Brother*, but the show he conceived would fit into today's lineup nonetheless.

In the end, Rogin's books deserve to be read and reread for one simple reason: They're funny. Along the way, feel free to be wowed by his pinballing imagination, his linguistic dexterity and his masterly ability to see clearly what is right in front of our faces but unnoticed until he pointed it out.

And what happened next to Rogin, after *Preparations?* Why did we not get a continuation of the story past middle-age and into dotage? In *About Town*, his 2000 history of the *New Yorker*, Ben Yagoda sums up Rogin's literary fate in, appropriately enough, a footnote: "Soon after publication of [*Preparations*], Rogin submitted two stories to [Roger] Angell, who told Rogin he was turning them down because they seemed to go over familiar ground. The criticism had a shattering effect on Rogin, and subsequently he has written no fiction."

Lowbrow Reader #7, 2009

In 2010, Verse Chorus Press returned What Happens Next? *and* Preparations for the Ascent *to publication in a new single-volume edition. Jennings's* Lowbrow *article served as the introduction.*

After being hipped to Gilbert Rogin's books through Jennings's essay, we were happy to meet the novelist himself, retired from the writing game and living down the street from Lowbrow *headquarters. In 2009, the* Lowbrow Reader *unveiled "My Masterpieces," the first Rogin story since 1980, written many years ago and published for the first time in issue #7.*

MY MASTERPIECES

by Gilbert Rogin

A LITTLE STILL life, an undistinguished arrangement of three cantaloupes looming over their mauve shadows, hangs on an otherwise bare wall of a hospital room. Just hours before, my wife (for years now my ex) had a hysterectomy. She has been brought down from the recovery room and is asleep, an outflung, almost beseeching, arm hooked up to the IV. Her face is a system of folds, as though it had been crumpled and then smoothed out, like an old love letter—one of mine to her, perhaps, reread, crushed, denied in a fist, and then, second thoughts....

As I keep my drowsy watch, my eye is drawn to the painting, which I hadn't noticed before. I approach it almost surreptitiously, as though with guilty foreknowledge. The signature is that of April Brown, whom I used to see many years earlier and have since forgotten. She lived on the sixth floor of a walk-up on Christopher Street.

This was long ago, before, seemingly one by one, my pubic hairs turned white. Her apartment was strewn with seashells she had idly picked up here and there—most quite ordinary but still affecting in their pale concordant mass—giving the impression that the sea had washed tumultuously through and then receded. As I would advance toward the bed on which she lay naked, artlessly disposed, I was willing to believe that the sea had delivered her, too, left her just so.

Examining the still life, I recall having once seen three cantaloupes on her kitchen table. She had halved one and we had it for lunch, possibly one of those she had painted; the shadows were her inspiration, the kitchen being illuminated by a fluorescent ring. *Ars longa, melo brevis.*

Most relationships between men and women are governed, in one proportion or another, by reason or sentiment; in those days, mine, on more than one occasion, were ruled by books— not their contents, their whereabouts. (A corollary: Often I can recall where I bought a given book, down to the shelf in the store, even its location on the shelf, long after I've forgotten its content. Much the same, I concede, could be said about my life. [This smacks of faux-profundity. Omit. *Ed.*]) That is, my affairs were cheerlessly prolonged because I had lent whichever woman a book and she hadn't returned it. My timing was always off; she was still on the wash cycle, so to speak, while I was on the rinse. Such was the case with April and the *Selected Letters of Madame de Sévigné*, which she was evidently memorizing. By the time I dug into my cantaloupe, feeling my spoon begin to bend, ominously prefiguring the deformation of my life, I had the desolate notion that we were connected by a life-support system. I steeled myself to pull the plug. She providentially went to the bathroom, where the tub crouched on its claw-feet like a forbearant beast; I glommed *Madame*, her place marked by a bakery ticket, off her bedside table, and fled, never to reascend those steep flights, my heart pounding, and then fling open the door to behold her, flecked with visionary foam.

A trick of time has made the cantaloupe whole, divided my attention. It is as if the still life is a window opening on the past, through which April wickedly beckons: LIVE NUDE WOMAN 25¢. I glance at my wife. Her eyes are open and she's watching me. I stand revealed, like an *écorché*, one of those anatomical figures from which the skin has been removed to disclose the muscles. If she had the strength to speak, she might address my treachery by saying, "Why?" To which I would feebly reply, "As has been said, the world wasn't imagined and constructed with the need for explanation in mind." I'm an ass.

....

Of everything that's changed—and, emphatically I include myself—Miami has been most rapidly and extensively altered. Of course, it may only seem that way. For tedious example, parents aren't as aware of the growth of their children as visiting aunts and uncles who exclaim, "My, how you've grown!" [A "tedious example" tediously exemplified. *Ed.*] This may be faintly Heisenbergian. I go to Miami four or five times a year; for all I know, Miamians who periodically visit New York may make the same assumptions about my city. Still, when I think that only a few years ago ibis diligently poked about the jungly tract before the Key Biscayne Hotel, where high-rises now stand, or how one evening, while I lay in Prudence Dunbar's bed in Coconut Grove, I saw through the window two monkeys gamboling in a tangerine tree (a Rousseauvian fancy realized), I feel I have the greater claim.

For that trip, Prudence had repainted her bedroom; she wanted to please me; she wanted me to marry her. When one day she came right out front and announced that I had said I would, I said I couldn't recall making such a statement. I wasn't shitting her; I couldn't. She cried all that night, and shortly afterward we split. I lost track of her for 15 years, while Miami underwent its great and wrenching changes (I'm put in mind of one of the transforming scene changes in *Götterdämmerung*). She was unaware of them, having, as I learned, married someone more steadfast, or less principled, than I, and moved to San Francisco. From time to time I recollected that night of anguish, how I had

Illustration by Doreen Kirchner

let her down, and was susceptible to renewed pangs of guilt.

When our paths recrossed, it was as though I had found a bottle on the beach in which the message was one I had written, confessing faithlessness—such as it was—and consigned to the currents. She and her husband had moved to New York and, quite by chance, rented an apartment almost next door.

We bumped into each other, had a drink in a neighborhood bar. A stuffed sailfish, painted lurid shades of blue and silver, arced in the gloom over the cash register, as if confident that one day the sea would seethe in and it could complete its astounding leap.

"You know," I said lamely, "I still feel bad about letting you down."

"What are you talking about?" she said, inexpertly groping in her glass for a segment of lime. It has been my lot to get mixed up with women who have as little manual dexterity as I have.

"That I led you to believe I'd marry you."

She laughed. "Oh that," she said. "I suppose it was under-handed, but I was desperate. I'd had it with Miami and wanted someone to carry me away from that Popsicle stand."

....

From my seat in the rear, the massed black yarmulkes of the mourners shine like the cobbles of a Hanseatic street at night after it has rained. This seems fitting (if a bit far-fetched); the names incised on the tablets framing the bimah denote that generations of German Jews have built and kept up the temple. Then a flash of white, like a scrap of paper agitated by a gust of wind that briefly catches the streetlight. A woman has momentarily turned her head. It's ——! What's she doing here? I hadn't known she had been acquainted with the deceased. [Trite locution. Fix! *Ed.*] I can't even recall her name. She was a friend of my wife's; we dog-sat for each other. When my wife and I went to Miami, she boarded our poodles, and when she went to—wherever, certainly more glamorous places—we took her puli.

One evening, when my wife had preceded me to Miami, it devolved upon me to deliver the dogs to ——. Why can I remember her apartment—linen shades and Louis legs—but not her name? Mandelstam said, "The living word does not designate any object, but freely chooses for its dwelling place, as it were, some objective significance, material thing, or beloved body. And the word wanders freely around the thing, like the soul around an abandoned, but not forgotten body." Not having an epistemological butterfly net with which to chase the little bugger down, swoop on it, let me just say that she lived on the sixth floor of a brownstone on Perry Street (how much wear and tear on my cardiovascular system I could have avoided if I had lived out my life, like certain species of monkeys, 60 feet up, and, ardent and agile, flitted from rooftop to rooftop), that it was snowing, and that as I mounted the stairs with an apricot mini tucked under each arm, I was prey to much the same emotions as when I traversed the switchbacks en route to April's.

The way it went, we started in on Mount Gay and Coke while the dogs roared through the chicanes and esses determined by the furniture legs. We must have eaten at some point because I recall trying to extract a last elusive strawberry from the depths of a parfait glass. More pops: shooters this time. Mildly amorous episodes. Letting the dogs out on the terrace, which was as white, silent, and illimitable as a dream of Russia.

Her bedroom was two steps up, a snug little unpainted shack of oak and cabin cedar built onto the terrace: her dacha. She lay on her stomach in the dark. I crouched, straddling her.

"What are you doing? Scratching my back?"

"No. Inscribing my memoirs."

"Hey, you're scribbling all over the joint. No one will ever be able to read it."

"As Heraclitus said, 'In writing, the course taken, straight or crooked, is one and the same.'"

Her back was broad, my life is long, I wrote devotedly and small, so I was at it much of the night.

Why did I feel the need to confess to my wife as we swam off Key Biscayne?

"What?" she said. "Take that goddamn snorkel out of your mouth so I can hear what the fuck you're saying."

"I said, 'But nothing happened.'"

"Sure," she said, "the two of you stayed up all night writing me love letters." She removed her wedding ring and flung it into the sea. She may be good hit—as, believe me, I can attest—but she's got no arm. I easily located the ring on the bottom a little way off, but it was like treasure recovered from a wreck, the flesh, the stiffening bone that penetrates the gold band, my life, less than dust.

....

Unable to sleep, I write with a forefinger on the bottom sheet a description of the various sounds made by the rain conjoining with the motel: sluicing, gurgling…and what? For though I bear down so hard one would have thought that not only the sheet, but also the mattress pad, the mattress, even the round, whirling earth would retain the impress, in the morning there is no trace. What had been the third participle—and had there been a Wordsworthian fourth and fifth? If, as has been said, language has benefited by the reluctance of things to be encased in it, can one also say that it is to the profit of things to withstand the predation of language? As I've indicated, this interested Mandelstam. "Is the thing really the master of the word?" he inquired. He couldn't leave it alone. "A word is not a thing," he contended elsewhere. "Its significance is not a translation of itself."

These speculations put me in mind of my late dad: the connection will become clear. Before I had resorted to furiously scribbling on the sheet, I had tried watching television. Changing channels, I had suddenly been presented with my dad's shapely hands, his rippling fingers. *Fantasie.* This godawful movie of the life of Schumann had once been a staple of late-night television, but now was rarely shown, and then nearer and nearer dawn; what with daylight seeping into the room, it seemed in fact to be fading away, its little light extinguished by the greater one of day.

If you've seen *Fantasie*, you will certainly recall that Paul Muni portrayed Schumann, Olivia de Havilland Clara, and possibly that José Iturbi played the piano. Only the most dedicated cineast will know that my dad supplied the hands. (A sad commentary on our Western value system; in Japan, I'm told, the name of the piano tuner is often printed in recital programs.) That is, in the close-ups of Schumann (Robert) at the keyboard, the disembodied fingers aren't Muni's or Iturbi's but my dad's. Muni, of course, couldn't play, and Iturbi couldn't be expected to sit there, pounding away under the lights, take after take. Enter my dad, fully, and somewhat ludicrously, costumed in case the young contract director who did the insert shots wanted, for example, cutaways of Schumann's feet soulfully pedaling.

A word about my dad, God bless him. He was a failed concert pianist. That is, after he moved to the coast in a largely vain attempt to make a fresh start, his concertizing was confined to performing at high school assemblies, with community orchestras, and at church services. He made ends meet by teaching and by playing cocktail piano at Ramada Inns. In a sense, his work on *Fantasie*, which he got because one of his brother-in-law's cousins was a *macher* at Warner's, was the high point of his career, and, herein lies the irony, so to speak. The piano he played on the insert stage was a dummy. That is (this, conspicuously, is a tale of "that ises"), it was rigged to produce no sound. Listening to playbacks of Iturbi's renditions of excerpts from *Carnaval* or *Davidsbündlertänze*, my dad showily depressed the keys in accord with Iturbi's interpretation. Thus, not one of my dad's notes has been preserved for posterity.

As you can see, an almost exact parallel can be drawn with my prosifying on ——'s back or the motel sheet or, for that matter, with the great work of invisible art I have been creating upon the canvas of America. Over the years, in a succession of rent cars, I have been undertaking a monumental painting. Assume the tires are rollers that apply pigment to the pavement as I ride over it. I do. Envision a map of the U.S. depicting only the roads, or segments of them, upon which I have driven, the colors more heavily laid down on those repeatedly traversed, and you will get an idea of my magnum opus if not the mood of the artist raptly or dreamily engaged in his work, smoothly ascending a flyover in Miami, his head cradled in the shoulder harness, Blasts from the Past blaring out of the quad speakers, reemphasizing a graceful curve, plunging down an off-ramp in Los Angeles, adding another sharp stroke to his composition.

Now let us regard my other great life's work, which stands in such vivid contrast to the foregoing or, rather, sits, as at present, on a motel bed in picturesque decay, looking down, as though into an abyss or in prayer or, like the fabled and sorrowing catoblepas, of which Pliny and Flaubert wrote, because my head is insufferably heavy. In fact I am contemplating my bare shins. These have become so scaly they resemble those of the Ratitae. Indeed, at age 50, I fear I am being transformed into one of those heterogenous beasts of legend—a chimera or hippogriff if not a catoblepas—for my face has grown so long and thin it appears nearly horselike. This alteration has been so gradual that my friends and associates have not remarked upon it, but one day soon a chambermaid, believing I'm out, will let herself in to do the room and, unexpectedly coming face to face with me, scream.

Did you know that the immense bones of Orestes, the discovery of which Herodotus relates, are now believed to be those of a prehistoric monster? Of course, the inference is not that Orestes had undergone a metamorphosis in his lifetime, one that was revealed from an examination of his remains; it is rather that the prevalent cult of heroic relics required outsized bones, and conveniently, those of great, lumbering Pleistocene beasts popped up from time to time. More persuasively, it was the other way round, as it often is, the uncovering of the bones leading to the formation of the cult.

But suppose the bones *were* Orestes's, that he became aware that he was in the grip of a terrible transformation, and that he was unhinged. Could that explain everything that followed? Something to think about early in the morning when your dad's ghostly, fluent fingers seem to be accompanying the rain.

Whatever, why have I become such a monstrosity? Allow me to lay the foundation. In television interviews in which only one camera is used, what are called reverses are a common technique. To explain. Obviously, for the most part the camera is focused on the subject while the interview is being conducted. To avoid monotony or having to resort to jump cuts, at the conclusion of the interview the cameraman then shoots the interviewer, who in rapid-fire order rattles off the same questions he has just asked, often negligently, in slightly different form. These reverses are then edited into the tape before the appropriate responses, so that in the interview you see on your TV screen, the answers have preceded the questions! What an imposture! What implications! You have a minute to dwell on them; I have been thus occupied for weeks. What keeps coming to mind is Heisenberg's description of a largely discredited scheme, a sort of time reversal in which "suddenly at some point in space particles are created, the energy of which is *later* provided by some other collision…between…particles at some other point." (Emphasis added.)

My incipient monstrosity may now be regarded in a different light. Instead of becoming less of what I was, I am becoming more of what I am.

Some propositions:

In a world of monsters, the aberrant or accidental human

would be designated a fabulous beast.

If horses and birds could imagine, they would find human characteristics in themselves.

Man, uniquely, has the power of imagining; he also, uniquely, has the power to imagine the worst of himself. God's trade-off?

Empiricism is an editorial process.

[I'm not sure if these are particularly trenchant. Reconsider. *Ed.*]

Heisenberg also wrote, famously, "What we observe is not nature itself, but nature exposed to our method of questioning." He wasn't talking about Miami or sailfish or even G.E. Moore's tree, but subatomic particles, which, as you know, by and large we cannot observe, pin down in the accepted sense; that is, we can determine their position or momentum, but not both simultaneously. And so return with me to words and things. A subatomic particle is not a thing, it is a tendency, a possibility, a *potentia*, in Aristotle's term. But what is a word if not an ambiguity straining to attain momentary discreteness—or resisting it. [Gil, give it up! *Ed.*]

And what am I, on the edge of a motel bed, on Heraclitus's road, unobservably, discontinuously, tending toward monstrousness? Schumann said (and Muni resonantly declaimed—a big scene), "The beginning is the main thing. When you have started, then the end comes, as if of itself, to meet you." But what's in between? Our knowledge of the system, the road, so to speak, whether it leads doggedly up the stairwells of brownstones or breathtakingly across rooftops, is incomplete, and for that reason each observation is irreversible. You only see me here, here, and here.

But *there*! I am idly watching *Fantasie* yet again. Schumann is in his parlor, playing *Davidsbündlertänze*, which he has just composed, for Chopin and Mendelssohn. Close-up of my dad's hands. After striking the twelfth of the low Cs that conclude the pieces, Schumann rises from the piano bench. Two-shot of Chopin and Mendelssohn applauding delightedly. The camera comes around for a reverse of Schumann from the back. He executes a little mock bow. The camera angle isn't precisely what the director wanted; for a fleeting moment Schumann's face is revealed, and I notice for the first time that it isn't Muni bowing, but my dad, and that he is grinning from ear to ear. Muni had the flu that day or he was in Chicago and they decided to cut corners and double my dad. As I watch Chopin and Mendelssohn give him a hand, I am touched to tears.

And *there* a chambermaid, stripping a bed of its bottom sheet, screams. She holds it up in astonishment. The sheet resembles a vast palimpsest or piece of intricate lace, so densely figured is it with words that seem to have burned the fabric away.

And, lastly, *there*, gazing out the window of an airplane, I see through a sudden rent in the cloud cover that the face of the earth has been transformed and now bears my resplendent and indelible mark.

....

It is my grandson Eddie's second birthday party. My daughter isn't speaking to her mother, my ex-wife, so there are only the three of us. I am in the kitchen, listening to country 'n' western on my clock radio and preparing filet of sole. My daughter is at the dinner table reading aloud our horoscopes from the *Post*. Eddie is standing in the kitchen doorway watching, transfixed, as I reverently sprinkle paprika on the gleaming fish.

"Dance, Eddie, dance," I tell him, turning up the volume.

"Dance, Eddie, dance," his mother tells him.

And Eddie dances in his tiny red sneakers.

I want to pluck Madame's letters from the shelf, call up April, and recite to her from where she left off on August 9, 1678 (the bakery ticket still marks her place, I've looked); write Prudence and compliment her for telling such an ingenious and consoling lie; make a last, glorious, dexterous swipe and pluck from the net ——'s name. What I would give to strip her to the waist, turn her around, and read on the hard, white page of her back what I wrote in the dark and have so utterly forgotten it might have been the unreconcilable circumstances of someone else's life.

....

With your indulgence, I will produce myself for the last time, a bedraggled rabbit from a tattered hat: The day preceding the night my daughter was conceived, my wife and I had been to the zoo and bought balloons, which we took home and let go so that they drifted to the ceiling, where, trailing their strings, they gently bumped. I recall that we remarked that there was a certain pathos about their attitude. As we were about to make love, I reached up, pulled them down, and tied the ends of the strings to my thing. Thus, giddy and buoyed.... High spirits leave their mark, too—*viz.*, a little dancing boy.

[Ah! *Ed.*]

CLOWNS AT WORK

by Neil Michael Hagerty

I HAVE LIMITED experience with clowns, but I also feel like I know a lot about them. In truth, like most people, I don't know much about clowns. And why should I? Clowns are redundant lore, unremarkable American scenery like teddy bears, tattoos or political cartoons. Clowns are among the foremost of the hundreds of cultural entities that have died but will not vanish. Their presence is perhaps expected in certain rare instances, but the clown is a run-down thing. Unless a clown has been theatrically postmodernized or abused and juxtaposed as a symbol in pop surrealism, one would barely bother to piss on the echo of its echo.

Historically, clowns have endured as allegedly essential to normal public life. In the 14th century, four blind clowns would come into town and chase a pig around with long sticks. You paid your money to see them strike each other. There is the tradition of the royal court jesters of England in the 15th century, the *commedia dell'arte* of the 16th century and the rise of the pantomime in the 19th century. The solo clown act of 20th-century America was a unique form that delivered an acceptable level of male pathos to a mass audience. This profound feeling actually resonated from the clown act itself, and not merely from the mortifying recognition of the weird choice one human being made to pursue clowning over everything else.

When I was a child, my father surprised me with tickets for a circus that was pulling into the arena where we would go to see basketball games. I wasn't a big fan of circuses; in fact, the only reason my dad got these tickets was to hand down to me an appreciation for a particular clown who was among the headline acts: Emmett Kelly. Kelly was incredibly famous during the classical period of the American clown, a period coinciding with the rise of television. In 1989, a decade after his death, he was a first-ballot inductee to Milwaukee's brand-new Clown Hall of Fame, opened just as the clown era was drawing to a close. (By the same logic, one could date a similar death of rock and roll to 1995, when the Rock and Roll Hall of Fame opened in Cleveland.)

In the language of the art form, Kelly was a tramp clown—as opposed to a white-face or rodeo clown. His character Weary Willie was based on the pathetic hobos spawned by the Great Depression. The act began with Kelly standing alone with a broom under a spotlight in the center ring—the sad janitor sweeping up after the circus for a few pennies. Kelly applied the broom to his own person, cracked a peanut with a sledgehammer, hung laundry on a low acrobatic wire and appeared to skillfully balance a delicate feather on his red nose while failing to juggle. Kelly reached down for a ball he had dropped, revealing that the feather's tip had been embedded into his plastic nose all along. What had appeared briefly magical had just been a low trick. Kelly's famous "sweeping the spotlight" bit closed the show. The clown attempted to sweep up the circle of light as it moved, grew in size and tripped him up until, finally, he forced it to dwindle and disappear into darkness. Kelly was the originator of this oft-imitated bit.

Despite the show having followed weeks of irritating hype from my dad, I must admit I was impressed by the size of the crowd, their fascination with Kelly and his command of their expectations. I am lucky to have seen Emmett Kelly in person. I have not seen a clown show since, but I know that there are thou-

Illustration by Alex Eben Meyer

sands of clowns out there, striving daily in this field that is dead in every way save as a vague archetype, working in this art form through which no artist might command national attention. In the hope of understanding this species a little better, I sent out a basic questionnaire to about 75 clowns. Two responded (see below). I have said almost enough. But I ask you to think again about clowns. They are out there. And they are working.

LOWBROW READER: What inspired you to pursue clowning?

LOU JOHNSON THE MAGICAL JUGGLER: To learn all those cool tricks like plate-spinning, stilt-walking and unicycling; at the same time, making people happy.

COCONUT THE CLOWN: I am an elementary-school teacher and decided to leave full-time teaching to pursue other ventures. They were offering a clown class through the recreation department in our city. The class was being held across the street from our home so I thought, Why not? That was in 1979. I have been clowning ever since. I am still a licensed elementary-school teacher, which adds to my credibility when I am booked for schools and libraries.

LOWBROW READER: What clown training or other types of education did you receive?

LOU JOHNSON THE MAGICAL JUGGLER: Ringling Bros. and Barnum & Bailey Clown College Class of 1990, Bachelor of Fun Arts. University of Maine at Orono 1993, B.A. in Theater/Dance.

COCONUT THE CLOWN: Like I mentioned above, a local class taught by two clowns, Sparkle and Slowpoke, who have become great lifelong friends. Also over the years, I have attended Clown College, Clown Camp, numerous conferences and conventions, winning awards for makeup on several occasions.

LOWBROW READER: What is your best or most popular routine?

LOU JOHNSON THE MAGICAL JUGGLER: Dick Zimmerman's Linking Hula-Hoops. I call my routine "Imagination." [Editor's Note: "Dick Zimmerman's Linking Hula-Hoops" is a variation on the classic "Chinese Linking Rings" illusion, wherein apparently solid rings are made to link and unlink at the magician's will. The "Hula-Hoops" variation utilizes the oversize plastic rings for comic effect and visual impact.]

COCONUT THE CLOWN: At the end of my show, I have a 16-pound bunny that jumps through a hoop. All the hoopla leading up to it makes the kids scream with laughter. The bunny really slips through the hoop to the delight of the audience. There's no jumping. It's all in the buildup.

For more information on Lou Johnson the Magical Juggler, call 516-599-2612 or visit www.loujuggler.com.

For more information on Coconut the Clown, call 303-425-0230 or visit www.coconuttheclown.com.

Lowbrow Reader #8, 2010

CURSES!

by Marsha Aronson Ruttenberg
Illustrations by Carl Cassel

M Y FATHER HAD a short fuse and a colorful tongue. Growing up, I believed that all parents enforced discipline with the assistance of Yiddish—and sometimes not-so-Yiddish—curses. I was convinced (with good reason, as I later discovered) that I would live to have children as obnoxious as I was; that if I made ugly faces my countenance would freeze into a freakish permanent state; that if I did not finish all the food on my plate, children in third-world countries would starve and die. When the need for more extreme expression arose, my father dipped into an old-shtetl repertoire both more distinctive and terrifying. Here are a few of his favorites.

Stick your head in the toilet three times
and take it out twice.

A streetcar should grow in your stomach
and you should spit transfers.

You should stick your head in the ground
and grow like an onion.

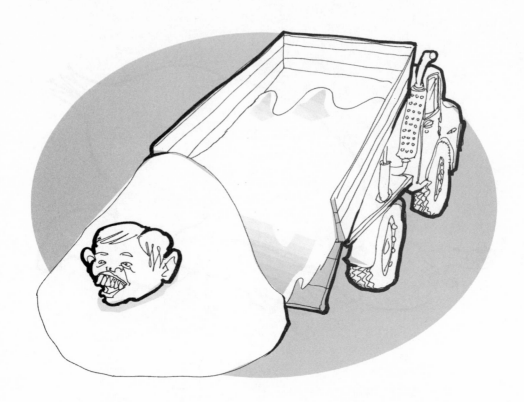

May your death be sweet—
you should be hit by a sugar truck.

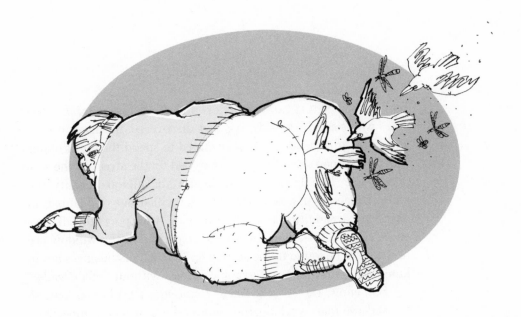

May vermin crawl up your ass
and lay eggs.

Lowbrow Reader #3, 2003

GENE WILDER:
THE MAGNETIC BLUR

by Jay Ruttenberg

THE FAVORED LOCAL video store's copy of *Young Frankenstein* was scratched—this, we had discovered the hard way—and so my girlfriend and I, determined to spend the night under Marty Feldman's deathly gaze, marched up the street to the second-choice shop. It's a filthy little store of dubious legality, the kind of place that was supposedly gentrified out of Manhattan years ago. In addition to renting movies, it purports to sell low-end electronics, though the goods advertised in the window are nowhere to be found in the store itself. Mostly, its business lies in kung fu arcana and pornographic movies without female leads.

Somehow, the store's *Young Frankenstein* DVD was out, so I asked the man working the counter—a storybook imbecile—whether he had a VHS copy. "Those are in *back*," he said irritably, as if "back" was code for "Afghanistan" or "the South Pole." An awkward silence ensued; finally, he sighed and embarked on his quest to the storage room.

The drunk idling by the counter recognized an opening to bother people and suddenly turned to me. "You look smart," he said. "Are you Italian?"

"That is the first time *that* sentence has ever been spoken," said my girlfriend, who is.

I told the man that I was not Italian. "You Jewish, then?" he asked.

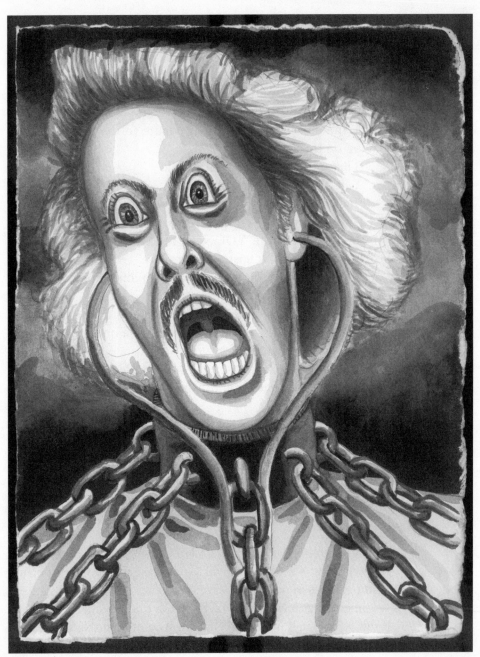

Illustration by Tom Sanford

"Yeah."

"You a doctor?"

"No."

"Oh," he said.

The three of us stood at the counter, waiting for the clerk to return with the movie. "Ya know, I saw the Clash once," the drunk announced, assumingly in tribute to the Ramones song playing on the store's radio.

"That must have been cool," I said.

"Yup. I like rock and roll."

Finally, the clerk returned to the counter clutching a battered VHS copy of *Young Frankenstein*. On the side of the box, somebody had written YOUNG FRANKENSTINE. "Here ya go," he announced. "It costs $3.25 to buy."

"Oh, I just want to rent it," I said, handing him four dollars. "I'll return it tomorrow."

The clerk's index finger punched something into the store's prehistoric computer. Then, he handed me a quarter in change. "Didn't you just say it was $3.25?" I asked.

The clerk grimaced. "It's $3.25 to *buy*. Renting costs $3.75."

"Wait—that means you're paying people to *not* return the movie."

"We're getting rid of our VHS tapes."

"I can see that," I said. "But why would anybody pay more money to rent a movie than to buy one? That's crazy! I could just buy it and throw the tape in the garbage after watching it."

"You *said* you wanted to rent it," the man huffed, aghast at the prospect of revising the invoice. "Now you're saying you want to buy it?"

Accordingly, I now own a VHS copy of *Young Frankenstein*. Although I was essentially paid to purchase the movie, its permanent presence in my tiny apartment makes me feel profligate—a sentiment that has caused me to watch the movie repeatedly, as if this will somehow compensate for its cluttering extravagance.

I long admired *Young Frankenstein* but considered it second-tier Mel Brooks, on par with *The Twelve Chairs* and *History of the World: Part I.* Through my guilt-riddled repeat viewings, however, the monster movie's quieter charms gradually made themselves known. Soon, a holy trinity of Mel Brooks—long obvious to most right-thinking people—gelled, in which the 1974 *Frankenstein* stands alongside the director's masterpiece (*Blazing Saddles,* also, astoundingly, from 1974) and legacy (*The Producers,* 1968). All three movies differ in tone and sensibility, yet all are united by one very potent force: their star, Gene Wilder.

For a comic, Wilder has a presence that is humble and soft—a marked and crucial contrast to Brooks, whose directing style could be compared to a farting elephant with a camera. Like a point guard celebrated for assists, Wilder often seems eager to steer attention to a fellow performer. Thus we think of Zero Mostel's blaring ogre in *The Producers,* Marty Feldman's bug-eyed cretin in *Young Frankenstein,* and the director's ensemble-driven bedlam (to say nothing of the dapper Richard Pryor stand-in Cleavon Little) in *Blazing Saddles.* Later, Wilder's polished generosity made him seem the ideal foil for Pryor—a harsh screen presence if ever there was one—in a string of buddy movies.

His screen appeal is vague, variable and strangely unaffected. Looking at *Young Frankenstein* upon its release, Pauline Kael found Wilder "a magnetic blur...born with a comic's fly-blown wig and the look of a reddish creature from outer space." Unlike most movie hysterics, his panic "seems perfectly natural. You never question what's driving him to it; his fits are lucid and total. They take him into a different dimension—he delivers what Harpo promised."

As with so many great performers, the twinkle-eyed actor's grace makes his job seem so easy that anyone thinks they can do it—even Matthew Broderick! One by one, Wilder's classic performances are adapted by lesser luminaries: Brooks famously revisited *The Producers* in a Broadway smash, with Broderick in Wilder's role; inevitably, that production spawned another movie, in 2005. That very year, *Willy Wonka & the Chocolate Factory*, Wilder's berserk slab of children's psychedelia from 1971, was remade, dreadfully, with Johnny Depp. And now, still basking in the green glow of his *Producers* musical, Brooks has brought *Young Frankenstein* to Broadway. How long before a chorus of bean-eating cowboys alights the Great White Way?

As Wilder's roles get expropriated and updated, you hold your breath, hoping the new versions will not drown out the original in history's mind, knowing full well that they never could. *Young Frankenstein*, especially—a film that Wilder conceived and co-wrote with Brooks—is a tour de force of slight ticks and mannerisms that ultimately eclipse its grander monster-spoof premise. Good luck and good riddance to those comers who dare attempt to fill these shoes! I, for one, am proud to own a copy of the original; it's well worth the money I was paid to buy it.

Lowbrow Reader #6, 2008

13 WAYS OF LOOKING AT GENE WILDER

(sorry, W.S. – I *said* I was sorry)
by M. Sweeney Lawless

1 Among twenty white coats,
The only still thing
Was the scalpel in the thigh.

2 I was of two minds,
Like Gene Wilder
It was Rhinoceros, but it was
also Zero Mostel.

3 The hair frizzled into a nimbus.
It was a premature equator of a part.

4 Gilda Radner
The Woman in Red.
Karen Wilder
See No Evil, Hear No Evil.

5 I do not know which to prefer,
The beauty of the mystery
Or the beauty of the appearance,
Willy Wonka limping
Or just after.

6 Partners Forever.

7 These are simple farmers.
These are people of the land.
The common clay of the New West.
You know, morons.

8 I know noble accents
And lucid, inescapable rhythms;
But I know, too,
We bad uh-huh.
We bad.

9 When the elevator smashed
through the roof,
It flew over the projection
Of London.

10 At the sight of her fiancé
In the huffing steam of the station,
Taffeta, darling
It wrinkles so easily.

11 He rode across the country
Coach.
Once, the compartment jarred him,
And he mistook
The mustachioed sleeper
For his wife.

12 The undertaker's car is moving.
Clyde must be driving.

13 He became Gene Wilder.
Because Jerry Silberman
Could not play Hamlet.
Then Gene Wilder
Could not play Hamlet.

Lowbrow Reader #6, 2008

THE TRAMPS OF PORDENONE

by Francesca Granata

S ALICE IS A small town in the northeast of Italy, so close to
the Baltics that natives flatten their Italian with slight
Slavic accents. Every October, the town is invaded by a
bespectacled pack of film scholars, journalists and archivists
for the Pordenone Silent Film Festival. Suddenly, the square's
provincial newsstand displays the *International Herald Tribune,*
Le Monde and the *Frankfurter Allgemeine* alongside *La Gazzetta*
dello Sport. Now in its 21st year—and 4th since moving to Salice
from its namesake city—the festival has become to the century-
old silent what Cannes is to the arty blockbuster. Nearly all of
the Pordenone stars, however, would have to be exhumed in
order to walk the red carpet.

This year, those ghouls would include Marion Davies,
Florence Vidor and Asta Nielsen—actresses celebrated for
their comedic roles at the festival, which was dedicated to
the oft-forgotten "funny ladies" of the silent era. Unlike their
better-known male counterparts, the comediennes generally
came from the stage, not the vaudeville circuit, and thus relied
less on slapstick than on traditional acting techniques.

Among the most prominent dramatic stars to slum in
comedy was Gloria Swanson. Her 1925 feature, *Stage Struck,*
portrays the diva against her glamorous image, as a diner wait-
ress harboring dreams of becoming an actress. Though popular

with contemporary festivalgoers, the picture was a 1920s flop both commercially and critically—so reviled that Swanson herself attempted to suppress the film. *Stage Struck*'s initial reception was possibly due to its artistic foresight: The movie opens with Swanson's character daydreaming about playing the very dramatic roles for which the actress herself was known. (Ironically, 25 years later Swanson concluded her career doing a similar—yet well-received—self-parody, in *Sunset Boulevard*.)

The comediennes' lack of elaborate Chaplinesque tricks hardly kept them away from embarrassing scenarios. Perhaps the funniest of the actresses showcased at Pordenone was Marion Davies, particularly in *The Patsy* (a King Vidor film from 1928). In the movie's most notorious scene, Davies eagerly makes herself the fool while impersonating a series of silent film divas—Mae Murray, Lillian Gish and Pola Negri—nailing their respective character traits with pitch-perfect accuracy. As

Marion Davies / Illustration by Doreen Kirchner

with Swanson, Davies is at her most potent when parodying the construction of glamour and her own "diva" image. Restrained to cerebral humor, the comediennes of Pordenone developed a self-reflexive comedy that seemed at once of its era and decades ahead of itself.

Lowbrow Reader #3, 2003

SILENT BUT DEAD

A Guide to the Lesser-Known Silent Comedians

by Jeff Ward
Illustrations by Mike Reddy

LOUIS L. LEWIS

If any comic of the 1920s is overdue for a revival, it's Lewis. A master of dialects and ethnic humor, "The Great Tongue" did peerless mimicry and double-talk, and his own upper-crust accent and rapid-fire delivery were trademarks. Unfortunately, he worked in silent movies. Lewis was convinced that audiences could follow what he said if he just enunciated clearly enough, which gave him the appearance of trying to dislodge peanut butter from the roof of his mouth. He was widely expected to do much better when sound came in, until the discovery, in 1929, that he wasn't funny.

NORMAN CLIVE

"Laurel & Hardy & Clive" were the princes of London's music halls and silent cinema. Of the three, the scene-stealer was Norm Clive, with his highly recognizable medium-size frame. A hilariously well-proportioned mesomorph, he kept crowds howling with his uproariously neutral personality. Ultimately, the apoplectically fat Hardy and passively skinny Laurel grew tired of

Harry Chester

competing with Clive's outrageous even-tempered appropriateness and sacked him, thereby depriving future generations of this incandescently average artist.

HARRY CHESTER

The ultimate milquetoast, Chester played cowardly bank clerks, icemen and Fuller Brush salesmen who, when intimidated, would urinate profusely on themselves. He was the best of the "incontinent clowns" who flourished under Sennett and Hal Roach. In private life, Chester was a ladies' man—he was married to Mabel Normand, Norma Shearer and, later, the indomitable Marie Dressler; the four shocked even 1920s Hollywood by living in open polygamy.

"TAFFY" PAYNE

The films of Charles "Taffy" Payne were pulled from circulation years ago, probably because his persona, a handicapped black homosexual, is triply offensive to modern sensibilities. But Payne's fame in the '20s eclipsed even Chaplin's. "To understand how popular he was," writes Leonard Maltin, "you have to imagine Julia Roberts *and* Arnold Schwarzenegger rolled into one, multiplied by chocolate orgasms." The suppression of Payne's films was accompanied by the ending of prejudice against the minority groups he portrayed.

JACK GIBSON

The most daring stunts of the silent age were performed by ex-wrestler Gibson. His first picture, *Hold My Pants*, featured jaw-dropping pratfalls, car crashes and blows from heavy objects, climaxing with a fall from the Flatiron Building that convinced some audience members that Gibson had actually died. (They were correct.)

PINKY CHALMERS

Although he stood only nine inches tall, Pinky Chalmers was a big star indeed. He would have been even bigger if Mutual had been able to find actors to use with him. They tried him first with Jackie Coogan, in 1922's *Lobster To-Day*, then paired him with a toddler, then a miniature schnauzer. His most enduring partner was Fuggles, a marmoset. Pinky's triumph, *Tiny Caesar*, contains the famous scene in which he hangs precariously from a grandfather clock. Pinky died in 1934 and was buried next to Valentino in a Bon-Ami can.

Jack Gibson

Pinky Chalmers

Lowbrow Reader #5, 2006

18 STORIES ABOUT CHRIS

by Michaelangelo Matos

M Y MOTHER USED to be married to a man named Chris. He wasn't bright, and he demonstrated this on a regular basis. Here are 18 recollections.

1. Chris drank a great deal. In fact, he was basically a drunk. So one day, when he and my mom were arguing, she told him so: "You're an alcoholic!" she yelled. "I'm not an alcoholic," he replied. "I've been drinking every day since I was 15—I'd know if I had a drinking problem!"

2. One day, Chris was feeling amorous. My sisters were then around 3 and 4 (he's their father) and I wasn't home, so he said to my mother, "Hey Lorie—let's send the kids O-U-T-S-I-D-E so we can fuck."

3. "You're stupid," my mother once said. "Oh yeah?" he retorted. "Well, you have the brains of two cents."

4. Another argument. "You're cold and unemotional," my mother accuses. "Well, what do you want me to do?" Chris answers. "I can't make my face turn into a heart."

5. One day, my Uncle James, Chris and I sat down for a game

of Trivial Pursuit. "I don't know if you should be playing this against me," Chris warned us. "You might be overmatched— I've got a college education." (Chris had gone to community college for six months, before dropping out.)

6. How do you get fired from a job? One way is to get extremely high and hit an elderly man with your car on the way out from your shift doing apartment maintenance.

7. Or how about this? Get hired as a butcher at Fuddruckers, where you work in a cooler behind a large glass window grinding meat; then, stand behind a side of beef and smoke pot in front of every person in the restaurant.

8. A couple of years ago, Chris paid a visit to my sisters, who are now 16 and 17. They were telling him about school—Alex, the older one, had recently won a footrace. "I could run faster than you with one leg tied behind my back," Chris said. Brittany looked him in the eye and said, "I'd like to see you try it." Alex, on the other hand, ran into the next room, crying, "Mom! He really does say those stupid things!"

9. One day when I was 13 or so, Chris was driving me to my great-great aunt's house in Minneapolis. (I lived in Richfield, a southern suburb.) He and my mother were separated and living apart, but still occasionally involved, and he would see my sisters every so often. In the car, he decided to have a man-to-man talk with me. A condensed transcript follows:

> "You know, you're getting to the age where you're starting to like girls. And pretty soon, you're going to start dating. And, well, you gotta be careful. Because you never know what'll happen. I mean, who knows? You might meet a woman, and start going out, and fall in love, and have kids, and get married, and get separated,

and get divorced, and end up paying fucking CHILD
SUPPORT!!!!!

Ahem. So be careful."

10. One summer day I was bored and possessed of enormous
goodwill. I decided to wash Chris's car. Being 8 and not knowing the first thing about washing cars, I used soap. Chris didn't
yell at me or anything, but I felt bad about my mistake, regardless. The next day, Chris and our neighbor Mike—who lived
down the hall and regularly beat his wife and stepson—went
out to the apartment parking lot to wash the car, this time
without soap. "Can I help you guys?" I asked. "That's all right,"
Chris said. "Washing a car is a man's job!" Then, he and Mike
exchanged a high-five.

11. Canterbury Downs is a racetrack near Minneapolis; soon
after it opened in the mid-'80s, my uncles James and Bob began
going regularly. One afternoon, they stopped by our apartment
before heading off to the track. "Why not make a couple sandwiches here before you head out?" my mom asked. Chris stormed
out of the bedroom, where he spent most of his time surrounded
by pot smoke. He had recently landed the Fuddruckers job, and
to celebrate had gone to the grocery store and bought some
lunch foods that he kept in separate compartments of the refrigerator and cupboards. I had been treated to a guided tour, during
which Chris pointed out which foods I was allowed to touch
and which I was to leave alone. (He didn't actually buy us food.
My mother fed me and my brother Jake—then a baby and now
deceased—on food stamps, while Chris kept his job money to
himself.) Now, with my uncles there, he yelled at my mom: "If
they use any of the food I bought for work I'm not buying any
diapers for the baby!" James and Bob took one look at each other
and ran into the kitchen to prepare their sandwiches. Chris
grumbled "fuck you" and stormed out of the house.

12. Naturally, Chris was a big wrestling fan. (This was in the mid-'80s, right around the time the WWF became popular.) In fact, Chris was such a big fan that he insisted the sport was legit. One afternoon, he got into an argument about this with

Illustration by Carl Cassel

my mother. A three-hour argument. I sat in my room with my ear to the door, listening and burying my face in a pillow so they would not hear my laughter. (Years later, my mother told me that during these arguments, she would move closer to my bedroom door so I could hear them better.) Finally, after three unceasing hours of debate, the unthinkable occurred: Chris broke down and agreed. "You're right," he finally said. "Professional wrestling isn't real. It's not like roller derby."[1]

13. "I don't believe you," Chris told my mother during another argument. "You lie like a kite!"

14. Chris once bemoaned the state of "young people today." (Chris, it should be noted, was two years younger than my mother, who gave birth to me when she was 14—which means he's in his mid-20s when all these stories occur.) "I remember when I was 10 years old," he said. "I was watching TV one day, and I thought, You know what? I'm bored. So during the commercial, I went outside, ran around Lake Calhoun, came back in the house, and got back on the couch just as the commercials were ending. I'd like to see kids do that these days." "So," my mom said, "what you're saying is that you ran around all of Lake Calhoun, which is at least a mile around, and came back in the space of a commercial? Chris, that's impossible! From your house to Lake Calhoun would have taken 10 minutes alone. Commercials are 2 minutes long, and the fastest man in the world ran a 2-minute mile." "Oh yeah?" he said. "Well fuck that fucking punk!"

15. "You know," he said one day, "when you say 'Christ,' you're really referring to me. Because my last name is Town and my

---

[1] Chris was far from the only stupid person my mother went out with. He was simply one in a very long line. Take Mike, a deeply dippy guy who once sat me on the kitchen counter and said, "You know why Mr. T has his name? Cause he's got a goat-TEE!"

first name is Chris, so you're saying *Chris T.* Christ."

16. One day, Chris and James went fishing; I tagged along. "Bring a can of corn," James advised Chris. "It makes good bait." So we drove an hour out to the spot, got out the tackle boxes and rods, and I said, "Hey, did you bring the corn?" (I was intrigued because I was 8 years old and had never heard of using corn for fish bait.) Chris nodded and whipped out a can of creamed corn. As he'd neglected to bring a can opener, his mistake turned out not be such a big deal, after all.

Illustration by Carl Cassel

17. Fourth of July, 1984. We decide to drive out to the woods and have a picnic. We make sandwiches, buy chips, fill a cooler with ice, soda, beer and Klondike Bars, and begin our one-hour journey. "The Klondike Bars all melted!" I cried when we opened the cooler. "So has all the ice!" "I told you not to put the cooler in the trunk," my mother scolded. "That's never fucking happened before!" Chris swore.

18. One day, driving the family to our great-great aunt's house, Chris took a wrong turn onto a one-way street. He avoided three oncoming cars and narrowly averted a collision with a parked one before finally making it down the block and turning the correct way. There was a minute of silence before my mother and I could finally breathe again. (My brother, who was less than a year old, was also in the car.) Suddenly, Chris beamed. "I must be the best driver in the world!" he exclaimed. "Anyone else would have gotten into an accident, but I avoided all those cars and none of us got hurt. I am one *great* fucking driver."

Lowbrow Reader #4, 2004

GO-GO-GO VON DUTCH:

The Strange Tale of the Now Gone, Though Not Much Lamented, *CARtoons* Magazine

by Neil Michael Hagerty

I REMEMBER *CARTOONS*

Across the street from Washington Irving Junior High School there stood a 7-11 store from which I would steal my extra-curricular reading materials. In a month, I might make three trips into this store for the purpose of procuring humor magazines. During the first, I'd grab the latest *MAD* and *National Lampoon;* on the second, *Crazy* and *Cracked;* if a third trip was needed, there, at the end of the rack, would sit my final quarry: *CARtoons,* the strangely beguiling, highly technical humor magazine devoted to the absurdity inherent in America's obsession with the automobile.

Unlike the *CARtoons* readership at large, my interest in this magazine was limited strictly to its satirical thrust, and while I could no more relate to its baroque punch lines, rendered in horsepower and torque, than I could relate to the oblique references to clitoral stimulation on the jokes page of *Playboy* (the one with the mutant nymph sprawled inside the cocktail glass—and yes, I knew what a cocktail glass was then, but that is a different story altogether), I found the grotesque art inspiring and the exaggeration of vehicular monomania satisfying enough to last until the new issue of *MAD* came out.

As time passed, *CARtoons* moved up on my theft list and

increasingly touched an amorphous frenzy inside me that had yet to be named. It was a magazine that, in some way, helped to transcend the psychosexual violence and resentful confusion that swarmed through the life of an American teenager.

CARtoons is gone now and not much lamented—perhaps endless variants on the melting engine joke proved replaceable over time. And yet, the tender element that the humor magazine crystallized in my soul stays with me to this day.

A BRIEF PUBLISHING HISTORY

CARtoons was created in 1959 by Pete Millar and Carl 'Unk' Kohler and was published by Trends books, which later turned into Petersen Publishing. But it was not until 1964 that the legendary "Unk and Them Varmints" was created. A brilliant synergy of fat street grease and exotic alien gremlins, "Unk" came to symbolize the possible epiphanies derived by conjoining elevated spiritual passion with automotive mechanics. Much the way Alfred E. Neuman represents that which is blithely seething in all of *MAD* magazine's content, "Unk and Them Varmints" finitely symbolized all that *CARtoons's* many and similar six-panel strips about four-engine ammonia-powered cars hoped to illuminate.

In 1975, *CARtoons* hit its stride with a revamping and rode the popularity of "gross" that permeated the decade (Wacky Packs, Odd Rods, Mad-Libs, Slime, etc....). It had a new logo, new artists and new features, including custom iron-ons and a "How To" section that led readers through drawing a particular car or truck. *CARtoons* began to destabilize in the '80s: The iron-ons went away in July 1983, only to come back in August 1984, and to disappear for good in April 1986. After that, there were color posters in the center; eventually, advertisements were introduced.

In August 1991, the last issue hit stands. There was no warning of its demise—it was just gone. Subscriptions to

CARtoons were changed to *Car Craft* for the remainder of the year and that was that. At its peak, Petersen also published *Teen, CYCLEtoons, SURFtoons, Hot Rod CARtoons* and more, though the three other "Toons" books closed by 1974. As a rather odd footnote, in 1997, Petersen Publishing sued Time Inc. over the rights to the name "Teen People," claiming it infringed on their mark "Teen." They lost this suit on appeal.

THE FLYING EYEBALL

Just as Marvel Comics had "Nuff Said" and *MAD* "What, Me Worry?" and "Potrzebie," *CARtoons* had recurring word marks that ran subliminally throughout the magazine, sometimes scrawled in the margins or printed on a sign in the background of a random strip panel. The most important of these word marks was "Von Dutch" (as in "Von Dutch is a dirty ol' myth" or "go-go-go Von Dutch"). Von Dutch is the key to understanding the essence of *CARtoons* humor.

Illustration by Doreen Kirchner

Von Dutch was a man. Born Kenny Howard, Von Dutch was *the* primal car-stripper and hot-rod customizer. He hand-embellished, brush stroke–by–brush stroke, the outer skin of custom machines, one by one, with painstaking and beautiful detail. When a car owner came to him, no one told Dutch what to do, but rather how much "time" he wanted to purchase. The designs were up to Dutch, and he pulled them from within the recesses of his soul (if such a thing can be said to exist). He had hundreds of imitators and followers, including Shakey Jake, the Barris Brothers, Tweetie, Slimbo and Ed "Big Daddy" Roth.

Von Dutch created the ubiquitous flying eyeball, which has been reappropriated infinitely and rivals the flying toaster and peace sign as a pathetic symbol harking back to an all-American moment of rebellion now lost forever, yet still dutifully encapsulated in consumer-friendly merchandise such as screen-savers or sink-daisies.

And yet, as is usual in these cases, there was an honest spirit behind the invention of this symbol: Von Dutch himself. He lived the Hot Rod credo in its purest state, expressing his life with colorful decorative finishes for over-stoked automobiles. Here is Von Dutch himself on the concept of money and the flying eyeball:

"The flying eyeball originated with the Macedonian and Egyptian cultures about 5,000 years ago. It was a symbol meaning 'the eye in the sky knows all and sees all.' I have always believed in reincarnation, and the eyeball was tied to that. I make a point of staying right at the edge of poverty. I don't have a pair of pants without a hole in them, and the only pair of boots I have are on my feet. I don't mess around with unnecessary stuff, so I don't need much money. I believe it's meant to be that way. There's a 'struggle' you have to go through, and if you make a lot of money it doesn't make the 'struggle' go away. It just makes it more complicated. If you keep poor, the struggle is simple."

The figure of Von Dutch is the archetype from which *CARtoons* evolved. The magazine was a serial replication of the Von Dutch modus, an attempt to characterize this form of spiritual devotion and replicate it in a linear and interactive manner for legions of car fanatics. Incidentally, the adoption of the humor-magazine format helped to attract readers who were seeking liberation through such satirical icons as the Cyclops-driven, jet engine–powered automobile.

CONTENTS & CONTRIBUTORS

Like the other humor magazines, *CARtoons* had a stable of freelancers who contributed throughout the publication's history. Their work in general was perhaps best characterized by Peter Bagge in reference to his own graphical style, which he described as resembling that of "a retarded garage mechanic tracing pictures out of an old issue of *CARtoons.*" Bagge's work is at least two or three ranks above that, but his reference in this instance is apt, and captures the spirit of the magazine's uniquely derivative content.

Some of its best remembered contributors include George Trosley, Nelson Dewey and Rick Griffin:

Trosley drew the "How-To" section and created the long-running feature-strip "Krass and Bernie," about a couple of dudes who lived in a room above a one-car garage. There was Bernie, the tall skinny guy, and Krass, his short sidekick, and they were both into only two things: cars and women. They could whip out a full custom car overnight, and still have time to go pick up some babes. "Krass and Bernie" was the first story in every issue, from February 1975 to the last issue in August 1991. Trosley also contributed to the *National Enquirer, Saturday Evening Post* and *Hustler.*

Nelson Dewey contributed gag pieces from issue #16 through the end. His style is instantly recognizable from "Stunt Dawgs," as well as *Readers' Digest* and *Oui.* He dealt with human-relationship scenes that took place in cars or involved disputes over cars.

Rick Griffin is perhaps best known from his later career as a psychedelic illustrator—he stole the flying eyeball logo in the late '60s for a poster he designed for Bill Graham's Fillmore. He also designed album covers for Neil Young (*On the Beach*), the Grateful Dead (*Aoxomoxoa, Wake of the Flood*) and the surf band the Challengers.

Other contributors of note included Joe Borer (who had a fine pencil-style), Willie Ito (who also drew *Flintstones* and *Josie and the Pussycats* animations), Shawn Kerri (whose cover drawing of the "Haunted Hot Rod" is a classic), Renfrew Klang, George Lemmons, Duane Bibby and Jerry Barnett, who later became an editorial cartoonist for the *Indianapolis News.*

LET'S LOOK AT AN ISSUE

Rather than let me read through an issue of *CARtoons* at its peak, I bid you to seek out your own copies from the prime era. I will instead focus on the roots of the magazine as it came to be known in its full flowering; these show clearly in its 20th issue (December 1964). The ideas are directed somewhat more pointedly at those familiar with automotive mechanics and the humor is lighter, yet the entire package points toward a future wherein would emerge the fully grotesque version of *CARtoons* that struck me innately despite the fact that I didn't know small block from large.

The cover shows "Unk and Them Varmints" in a situation described thusly: "It's the night before Christmas and all around the Timing Stand them Varmints are waiting to decorate the Chrondek Tree that one lil' rowdy Varmint has just chopped down...to Unk's dismay."

The inside cover features an installment of a continuing strip called "Ham Bones," by Lemmons. Here we see two speed enthusiasts heading to the famous Bonneville Salt Flats. One of the ham bones wears a folded-brim jalopy cap; the other has thick features and sports a crew cut. They debate the merits of using smaller or larger bored-out jets on their super car. The punch line revolves around a melted engine. Later in the issue, Willie Ito and Carl Kohler revisit the Salt Flats. In their tale, visiting enthusiasts are preyed upon by an old man in a magnetically-powered hovercraft. A variant of the thieving-troll archetype, he comes out at night and steals car parts; he receives his comeuppance at the end of the seven-page story.

The letters page ("Dear Unk") features *MAD*-style sarcastic replies from the editor to the hapless correspondent. For example:

> In my block everyone digs your magazine. We're waiting for someone to bury it. –Dennis Olson, Austin, Texas

> *I didn't know you Texas-types could read.*

A six-panel strip entitled "A-Doorable" offers a take on the theme of a large man emerging from a small car. A misunderstanding arises after an accident. One man rips away the door of the other's car in anger and then realizes that the man inside is huge and muscular. The smaller man is seen in the last panel with a welder, reattaching the door he had previously ripped off.

Four pages of "Unk and Them Varmints" follow. This tale relates how the Varmints dislike using public transportation; in order to satisfy Unk's demand that they "ride the bus," the Varmints buy a souped-up bus that Unk can't resist. Featured in this strip are two other word marks used by *CARtoons:* "Hooray for Schmeerps" and a general exclamation, "Moogaloonie!"

"Show Me the Way to Go Chrome" is a six-panel strip dealing with class warfare. A slob and his jalopy are derided by a lockjawed swell at a car show. Later, the slob's jalopy is shown surrounded by car-show trophies, and the swell can't believe it. We learn how the jalopy got all those trophies when the slob is seen removing a saw from his front seat; he enters the basement beneath the trophy room ("Von Dutch Forever!" is written on the basement door) and in the last panel we see him sawing out a circle around the first-place trophy from below.

Nelson Dewey's "Pink Slip Passenger" is a cautionary tale about a man who becomes exasperated by his date's backseat driving and gives her the wheel. She then proceeds to race a carload of women she sees at a stoplight as the man hangs on helplessly. They get pulled over.

Renfrew Klang's "A'la Kart" runs four pages and tells the story of two street go-karters who get busted by the fuzz everywhere they ride. Eventually, they attach lawnmower blades to their karts and ride on lawns (rides for which they get paid, as the approving cop duly notes).

"Foto-Funnies" are certainly a venerable humor magazine feature, and *CARtoons* naturally made use of them. Issue #20 has several pages of uncredited Foto-Funnies: The first two feature antiquated vehicles and drivers to heighten the sense of the ridiculous, as well as slang-ridden, incongruous captions that draw humor from anachronistic juxtapositions. The last installment doubles back on its own concept, just as the reader is becoming inured to it, by using old science-fiction movie stills featuring cars and robots. Another photo feature, by Lynn Wineland, details the specs of a fictitious "Spirit" LSR car in a parody of real car magazines, such as *HotRod* or *Chevy High Performance.*

As this is the December issue, four pages are dedicated to "A Visit from St. Nicholas, 1964." This parody poem (with accompanying illustrations) transforms the old holiday doggerel by having Santa fly in a hot-rodded drag-sled as he visits the denizens of "Bob Ratchet's Rod Club" who are nestled snug in their cots dreaming of "chrome axles and four-barreled pots" until they are awakened by Santa's screaming engine.

Rick Griffin makes an appearance with a four-page story about "Hapless Hank," who takes so long to build a custom woodie that by the time he finishes with it, woodies have gone out of style. In a similar vein is Harry G. Harley's three-page "Small Changes," where two customizers get so carried away rebuilding an old jalopy that they forget to install an engine. The final depiction of their car hints at the exaggerated anthropomorphizing that would soon dominate the pages of *CARtoons*.

Perhaps weirdest of all is Jim Grube's "Unsanctioned," which tells the story of two friends who have an adventure at an unsanctioned drag-strip that features a dog as tech inspector, Fidel Castro as track official and Frankenstein's monster as security. The race is won by a bucktoothed villain in a Dr. Seuss–style hat, when he uses a hand grenade to blow up the competition.

IN CLOSING

The back cover of issue #20 says it all: "Wanna Start Sumpin' Wild?" And although the writers are referring to a picture of a hand-cranked engine (and the possibility of buying a subscription to *CARtoons* itself), they are also inviting the uninitiated to enter the chaos of purifying obsession. In the sense that *CARtoons* reflected, contained and evolved this obsession through its own grotesque satire, I would say that it was a pretty good magazine and well worth stealing. Or, as one letter-writer put it:

> *WHO is Von Dutch and WHERE is he? Even more important, WHAT'S an Unk Kohler and HOW did it get off Java Jetty? Gotta go now, I'm adjusting for skim on my slot-rod. It's 'Help Stomp on Varmints Week.'*

> *Lowbrow Reader #1, 2001*

LETTER FROM THE EDITOR:
TO THE ALUMNI

by Jay Ruttenberg

U NDER AN ANGRY New England sky, Barth University held
its 179th commencement in a damp yet picturesque May
ceremony. Honored attendees included last-minute commencement speaker Jim Belushi, who urged graduates to "make like
Southern Italians" and defer the responsibilities of the working
world for "a number" of years, and valedictorian Joan Wright,
who lost her voice on graduation morning but, through swiftly
learned sign language, delivered an impassioned sermon cau-
tioning her fellow graduates against partaking in strident bar-
room debates the night before important speaking engagements.
Presented with honorary degrees were Paul S. Suggs, who last
year patented a unique method of navigating the New York City
grid using only the scents of vending carts and clicks of traffic
lights; Dr. Heather Usher, a celebrated botanist, hunter and *Jane*
magazine columnist; and Willie Smith, an American Indian.

We extend congratulations to Jody Sampson (A '91) and
Steven Carpenter (A '99), who were married last February in
a beautiful North Carolina service faultless but for the now-
infamous altar protestations of the father of Mr. Carpenter's
lover (A '74) and a very brief attack of nonpoisonous hornets.
Barth University alumni attending the wedding were, from left:
Abe Libman (E '99); Robert Swell (A '98; since deceased); groom
(with tie); Sarah Pasternaker (A '93); Matthew Shaw (E '93;

in wheelchair); and Margaret Thorne (A '99; since deceased). (Bride, not pictured.)

Faculty in the news: Professor Arnold Helman, chair of Barth's nutrition department, recently published his fourth book, *Ice Cream: Not Just for Fatsos Anymore!* (Xlibris), a scientific defense of the pre-supper Ice Cream Sundae. Also recently published are American studies professor Van Crowley—whose *9/11* examines the lives of 82 Barth undergraduates with birthdays falling on September 11—and music adjunct Frank Christopher, whose shrewd analysis of the lyrics of ballad powerhouse Diane Warren won this year's coveted Diane Warren Music Writing Award.

Illustration by Mike Reddy

Ships ahoy! In August, Barth's two oldest living alumni, Zachary Pernice (A '69) and David Loggins (A '70) set sail on a Bahamas cruise. While the cruise was ultimately cut short due to the persistent meddling of a glamorous young band of pirates inspired by the Johnny Depp blockbuster, our silvery graduates found time to reminisce about Barth's '60s days. "Things around the college were different back then," Pernice noted.

We are sad to report the death of Dr. Tony Greer, D.D.S., former co-chair of the university's dental program and a founder of UScareUK, a humanitarian exchange program in which American dentists travel across Great Britain providing free care to those in need. An active and often divisive member of the Barth community, Dr. Greer—who quietly passed away during the night after falling asleep on a butcher knife—will be remembered for his tireless lectures on flossing and heroic attempts to hump Patrice Tauber, Ph.D., president of our university's award-winning nursing program.

Older alumni may recall that, prior to the university's fateful 1999 decision to go public on NASDAQ, this space of the newsletter was devoted to the solicitation of charitable donations. This month, we reintroduce the feature, as the greater Barth family comes to the financial aid of beloved poetry professor Charles O'Malley. A decorated veteran of World War II, where he won a Presidential Medal of Honor for his work writing clever sayings on the sides of bombs, Professor O'Malley recently contracted pneumonia while marching in protest of what he deemed an inadequate university health care plan. Naturally, his insurer refuses to cover all subsequent hospital bills. An assumed homosexual, Professor O'Malley has no children to foot his medical bills and bring him the flowers one would guess he so dearly loves. We ask all alumni who were touched by this great man to help him in this time of need. (Cash only, please.)

A VISIT WITH
OL' DIRTY BASTARD
by Margeaux Rawson

E ARLY IN 2004, entertainment journalist Margeaux Rawson bravely entered the Brooklyn brownstone of rapper Ol' Dirty Bastard to interview him for a magazine piece. Needless to say, the troubled Wu-Tang Clan star was hardly a loquacious interview subject, foiling plans for a substantive article. *Lowbrow* seized on this rare opportunity to blow the whistle on the state of Ol' Dirty's fingernails, furnishings and renowned aroma. Months after the article's publication, the rapper died of an accidental drug overdose.

LOWBROW READER: You're probably one of the few women who has been inside Ol' Dirty Bastard's house and hasn't returned with a venereal disease.

MARGEAUX RAWSON: Or a child.

LOWBROW READER: Where does he live?

RAWSON: He lives in Brooklyn. It's an odd location—it's not ghetto-ish, but it's also not where you'd expect a star to live. In Brooklyn, most stars live in Brooklyn Heights, Williamsburg or Fort Greene. But he's in more of a working class, family neighborhood. A lot of brownstones and row houses; it's not near a subway or an urban center.

LOWBROW READER: What's his house like?

RAWSON: He lives in a brownstone. It's been renovated, so it's modern on the inside. It's a narrow apartment, with white walls and hardwood floors. It's surprisingly well-kept and pretty neat—except for its smell. It smelled *bad*.

LOWBROW READER: Can you describe the odor?

RAWSON: It was the smell of Newport cigarettes, feet, ass, food and unbrushed teeth. Just all-around *funk*. A bouquet of stink.

LOWBROW READER: So you get to his house and what happens? Did you have to take your shoes off at the door?

RAWSON: No, no shoes off. Nothing like that. I got there and his manager met me at the door. There was another reporter there, from *Rolling Stone*, finishing an interview. We walked past Dirty's bedroom, which was right up front on the first floor—it's kind of a weird place for a bedroom.

LOWBROW READER: What was in his room?

RAWSON: Not much. A raised bed; wrought-iron frame. I'm not going to say it was nice bedding for him, but it was okay. It was tacky in that rapper-thinks-it's-nice kind of way. I want to say it was a colorful spread—somewhere between fuchsia and burgundy, with a paisley-swirl kind of thing going on. There was some type of canopy situation involved. We continued walking down the hallway, past a small, narrow kitchen. Again, it was oddly neat, and nothing was on the walls.

LOWBROW READER: No Wu-Tang Clan memorabilia?

Illustration by Mike Reddy

RAWSON: No—nothing. Just white walls all around. Offset from the kitchen is the living room and the dining room, and both were quite small. The dining room just had a table and chairs, and the living room had red leather couches. Very *New Jack City*. I went into the living room and there he was: Ol' Dirty Bastard. Sitting in a bathrobe.

LOWBROW READER: Was it a ratty robe?

RAWSON: It wasn't the nicest robe I've ever seen. It wasn't like George Hamilton or Hugh Hefner in a smoking jacket. It was more like a bathrobe from Marshalls. Velveteen or terry cloth, with gray and black stripes. And he had no shirt on underneath it. He also had on jeans—and the legs were pulled up so you could see that he had sweatpants on underneath the jeans. It seemed to me that he slept in the sweatpants and then pulled some jeans on over them. He had on these brown pleather slippers, so you could see his heels, which were ashen. His feet looked *nasty*. And his fingernails were long, like Barbra Streisand's, and caked with dirt. They were black—blackety black.

LOWBROW READER: Tell me about the interview.

RAWSON: The moment of truth! The first thing he said to me was, "This ain't gonna be long, aright?" So I was like, "Okay— what have you been up to lately?" And he said, "I'm just trying to get money. That's all I'm trying to do." I went on asking him questions, because this was supposed to fill up an entire page of Q&A. But he just replied with one-word answers—after all the "ums" and "you know what I'm sayings," they were just one word. And it was usually "money." I said, "You seem to be living okay right now—what more do you need?" And he just screamed "Money!" I said, "What kind of money do you want?" And he said, "Millions." And then his manger said, "Fuck millions—you want billions." The manager kind of disturbed me.

LOWBROW READER: Why is that? What's the manager like?

RAWSON: He's this white guy named Jared who kept making jokes about how he's a greedy Jew. It's really sad. If I stopped to ask the manager a question—like, "Why can't he speak in full sentences?"—Ol' Dirty would fall asleep. And the manager would have to scream to get his attention: *Dirty! Dirty!*

LOWBROW READER: Wasn't there a lady there, too?

RAWSON: Yes, there *was* a lady. I forgot about the lady. She was an overweight white woman who was quite…trailer park in her appearance. Bad perm or frizzled hair. She was very "street" with her mannerisms. She sat with her legs wide open and her arm sprawled on the chair. She was wearing jeans and a jersey, or some such urban apparel—she was pretty hardcore.

LOWBROW READER: Was she touching him at all?

RAWSON: She wasn't touching him. But at one point in the interview, I asked ODB to talk about the ladies in his life and he told me, "I ain't got no ladies." She seemed visibly disturbed by that response. There was no purpose for her to be hanging out during the interview—she just seemed to be the lady of that day. Judging by her body language, she seemed to be trying to tell me, *I'm the lady of this house!* And that's fine with me—I'm not stealing Dirty anytime soon.

Lowbrow Reader #4, 2004

AN EXCERPT FROM MARGEAUX RAWSON'S INTERVIEW WITH OL' DIRTY BASTARD

MARGEAUX RAWSON: Is everything okay between you and the other members of the Wu-Tang Clan?

OL' DIRTY BASTARD: Yeah.

RAWSON: I thought you were upset because a lot of them didn't visit you when you were locked up.

ODB: Nah. I wasn't upset.

RAWSON: How did you feel when they got Flavor Flav to appear in your place on the last album, when you were in prison?

ODB: I wasn't upset.

RAWSON: Since you've been on parole, you've been doing a lot of shows and recording. How do you fit all that into your schedule given the time constraints of your parole?

ODB: I just fit it all in.

RAWSON: You know, this interview is for a full-page Q&A, so I need more than one-word and one-sentence answers in order to make it work.

ODB: That's all I can do, man. I don't even know about no two-word answers. I don't know how to get down like that. That's how I talk.

RAWSON: You're just a concise speaker.

ODB: Yeah.

RAWSON: Let's talk about the ladies in your life.

ODB: I ain't got no ladies in my life.

RAWSON: Well, what *is* in your life? What are you excited about right now? What is your passion?

ODB: Just money.

RAWSON: Why is that?

ODB: Cause that's all I can use right now. I don't know what else to use right now.

RAWSON: Is there anything you haven't done that you would like to do?

ODB: Get out America and go live somewhere else.

RAWSON: Where?

ODB: Somewhere far. I don't know.

RAWSON: Why do you want to leave America?

ODB: Cause I don't like America.

RAWSON: Why? What do you dislike about it?

ODB: The government—how they do things.

RAWSON: Do you feel wronged by the government?

ODB: Nah. I just don't like America. That's all, you know what I'm saying? I want to go somewhere else. When you lived in America all your life, you just want to get out America.

RAWSON: Would you want anyone to go with you, like your kids?

ODB: Nah, just me by myself.

RAWSON: Are you close to your kids?

ODB: Yeah.

RAWSON: So why wouldn't you want them to go with you?

ODB: Cause I just want to do things for myself.

RAWSON: Do you want to start all over?

ODB: Yeah.

RAWSON: That's interesting. How do you envision your life would be if you could start all over?

ODB: I ain't tryin' to start all over. I'm just tryin' to get out of here. That's all.

RAWSON: If you were the president, what would you do differently?

ODB: I wouldn't do nuthin'. I would grow old.

RAWSON: Do you feel fulfilled and satisfied?

ODB: Nah.

RAWSON: Why not?

ODB: Cause I gotta get that money.

RAWSON: More money?

ODB: Yeah.

RAWSON: You seem to be living okay right now—what more do you need?

ODB: Money!

JARED THE MANAGER: You know people. No one ever has enough money. Bill Gates wants more money; Ol' Dirty Bastard wants more money.

Lowbrow Reader #4, 2004

IS THIS SOUP ATKINS KOSHER?
Dating Jackie Mason

by Liza Weisstuch

M Y FAMILY HAS always wanted me to meet a nice Jewish boy.
And indeed, Jackie Mason was, years ago, a nice Jewish
boy. But that was some time ago, and I doubt that my Bubbe
would have been very proud if she had known, when I told her
that I met Mr. Mason, that I actually meant we had gone out
on a date. What else is it when a man takes you to a restaurant,
buys you a salad and talks about having sex?

Jackie is touring his show *Much Ado About Everything* when
we meet. This is a good thing, as I don't know if I would feel as
comfortable recounting this story if it happened the following
year, when he was touring a little number tagged *Prune Danish*.
(I'm no publicist, but I can think of a few slogans for that one,
not a few of which involve the word "running.")

As legend and census both have it, there aren't as many
Jews in New England as there are in New York, but it's as hard
to believe now as when I first see Mason, lumbering through
Boston's Copley Square by himself, that I would be the only
person to approach him. His shoulders are scrunched in their
hallmark shlump, his bottom lip juts out to give him a look
that's part pensive, part baffled, part grimacing. He doesn't so
much stroll as trundle. His walk is as staccato as his speaking
voice—and his famous tripping-over-words accentuated-by-
jagged-gestures appears to be no mere schtick.

I already know that he is in town this weekend because of my job, covering theater for some Boston papers. I spot him immediately—despite his small stature, he isn't hard to spot if you've ever seen an image of his legendary mug. What he lacks in physique he makes up for with whatever you'd like to guess you know about him. He'll tell you it's a typical drawback of being a celebrity with tenure—everybody thinks they know you personally. Besides, isn't it in an icon's nature to disappoint with actual stature when you're in his presence?

I approach and Jackie is noticeably bowled over that a woman one-third his age recognizes him. But number-wise, conjecture dominates. (The only time he ever becomes visibly angry with me is when I eventually ask how old he is.) We start talking. I introduce myself, he introduces himself, I tell him he needs no introduction. Jackie never seems ready to quit talking, so he takes me to lunch. We dip into a little Italian joint on the tony side of Newbury Street; on the way, he asks if I want to go back to his hotel. I order a salad, he orders a pasta dish. He's trying to stick to the Atkins diet, but he just can't. He asks the waiter whether soup is good for the Atkins diet. The waiter doesn't know. The waiter walks away and Jackie calls him a putz.

Dining with Jackie is like falling into an Old World Jewish fortune cookie. Imagine unspooling a Dead Sea Scroll of Yiddish-inflected commentary from the inner helix of a rugelach: *The fancier the restaurant, the more you pay and the less you get.... First people exercised by running. Then as a nation, we were commanded to power walk, so we power walked. Then we learned that just walking was fine. Pretty soon, these schmucks will just stand still.... Cellphones are shrinking and people are self-righteous about the diminutive scale of their own phones, they feel superior when they confront someone whose phone is bigger.... He's never been married, never had children.... He doesn't want to make me uncomfortable, but he feels it necessary to point out that we've talked about everything but sex.*

"What are you, frigid or something?"

"It's not that I'm frigid, Jackie—I just don't know whose sex

Illustration by Tom Sanford

you want to talk about," I tell him, careful not to reveal what I'm really thinking, that celebrities are the most dubious species of humans with whom to have a tryst. How do I know that he doesn't have a bunch of Chinese immigrants stashed in his hotel closet? How do I know he doesn't have a sleeping pill habit? And what I'm most specifically thinking as he wipes a speck of spaghetti sauce from his cheek is: *Gross!*

"You're right, you know. In this day and age, it's not good to rush off and sleep with someone after only knowing him for a day and a half," Jackie concedes. "I respect that you don't want to come back with me and take all your clothes off. I mulled over having an affair with you, but I sensed from the beginning that you were self-conscious about it. When I bring it up, you change the subject. Are you self-conscious about it?"

"I guess I'm a little self-conscious about it. I guess so, yes." Not too conscious of my own self, as much as *his* self, I failed to clarify.

All this is coming from the comic legend who makes it known in his schtick that he doesn't like to talk about sex in public. Well, here we are in public. But he feels better, now that he doesn't have to wonder where things are going. I'm entitled to feel the way I feel. (Geez, thanks, Jackie. How'd he know I've always wanted a man who wouldn't disenfranchise me?)

Maybe, he says, I just don't find him attractive. Maybe there is a problem with the age difference. It's quite apparent that this is a matter of self-consciousness for him. He never broaches his age onstage. Ask him how old he is and he'll tell you he's 26. Or he'll get angry and call you rude.

He tells me, as he's told numerous audiences, that he is an "obsessive egomaniac" and proud of it. He can joke and joke, but after a date with Jackie Mason, you walk away with a cloud of sadness hanging over you like the belly sags over his belt line. He's the archetypal portrait of a man who devoted his life to his work at the cost of having nobody to be with him as he moves from hotel room to stage to hotel room. When he's offstage, he tells me, he spends his time reading, writing, watching the commentators on television.

He pays for the meal and we walk back toward the Shubert Theatre, where he is performing later that night. It's 6:30. A woman frantically approaches him outside the theater. There's a slight chill settling in the air, but she has been sweating. She has the frazzled air of a mother looking for her son's missing dog. She addresses Jackie in a scolding tone. He goes pallid as he looks at his watch. He's late—he thought the show was at 8:00. Nobody stops me, so I accompany them as she ushers the comedian to his dressing room. As someone cakes makeup on Jackie's face, he instructs me to meet him in the morning. He asks me if I want to stay for the show. I wonder if that means backstage. There's an appealing plate of fruit next to the makeup. Sure, I tell him, so he calls to the woman, who has blotted her own face by now.

Then he realizes tomorrow is Sunday. What was he thinking, trying to meet on a Sunday morning? On Sunday mornings, while Jews across the country schmear their bagels with thick globs of cream cheese, the silken bedding upon which to lay the soft pink lox, Jackie Mason watches political pundits and commentators talk about the state of the union, the decline of morality, the abominable state of fraudulence among people in power, and how they get off on vilifying others. It's sick. It all, he says, makes him "nauseous."

But it's the stuff he builds his livelihood upon. He's critical, cynical, harsh and unforgiving, but he's a real softie not too deep underneath.

The woman escorts me to a seat in the balcony. I applaud with everyone else when he steps onto the stage.

I still think about the time I looked deep into the sex-starved eyes of Jackie Mason, across a table of salad and pasta, white bread and water. I saw the soul of a man longing for human companionship, for someone who would talk about things that lie beyond the morning news headlines, things to offset the scathing kvetching that is his hallmark. He can say as much as he wants as often as he wants to convey the impression that he's a hard-shelled disparager of the sorry, cynical state of human nature. But when you strip it all away—and no, I don't mean *that*—when you take away the name, the merchandise, the archives, the trademark shrug and hand thrusts, he's just like any lonely old guy who looks back on his life with regret.

Lowbrow Reader #4, 2004

WHAT DO I LOOK LIKE, HENNY YOUNGMAN?

About the Reissue of
Lou Reed Live: *Take No Prisoners*

by Neil Michael Hagerty

W E AMERICANS HAVE always politely pretended not to com-
prehend Cockney slang out of respect to the cultural
code of a fondly admired underclass. We perceive immediately
the construct of Cockney slang, but each time we hear it, we
shrug and twist our faces into the best confused looks we can
fake. As with French rappers or Swedish neo-fascists, we cede
to Europe its tradition and ancient mystery, we doff our beaver
caps to them, and we move on.

And so it was that when Lou Reed was christened "man
of letters" by the Royal Academies of Europe, Americans
responded by respectfully ceasing to buy or listen to his music.

But now is the time for all good people to come to the aid
of our countryman. *Take No Prisoners*, a live LP recorded in
Lou Reed's New York and originally issued in 1978, has been
released on CD for the first time and should be reconsidered and
purchased, perhaps to provide a sort of ransom to his captors so
that he may be returned to the United States—especially now,
when we could use some information about fear and confronta-
tion and the positive possibilities of the failed agenda.

In an American vein, like the lines on your palm, look back
across time to the solid sales statistics and credentials of Lou
Reed. From 1972 to 1974 he charted three LPs at 29, 45 and 10,
and he had one very large high-charting single that has become

a staple of classic-rock radio and samplers (both kinds). Around that time he also released three counter-popular "masterpieces" including an electronically generated portrait of amphetamine chemistry.

In the '80s, he produced at least two high-charting LPs that I can remember and contributed a song to *Perfect*, a *Rolling Stone* magazine–based lifestyle film concerning aerobics that starred Jamie Lee Curtis and John Travolta. He shared a duet with either Sam or Dave (I think it was Sam) on a new version of "Soul Man," which was used as the title song to a film about a young Euro-American man who pretended to be a young African-American man in order to gain admission to a certain college. (I smell a Jack Black remake!) Reed was also featured in a series of commercials for a Japanese motorcycle.

Recorded at the Bottom Line over a series of evenings toward the end of the '70s, *Take No Prisoners* is a terrific album. It has many of Reed's best-known songs (albeit in highly altered forms) and a lot of energy. But it is important to look at *Take No Prisoners* from beyond the confines of Lou Reed's rock stardom and not to dwell on the puerile interest that was once generated by the polymorphously perverse and decadent world from which it supposedly emerged, with its local and exclusive references, Diana Ross name-dropping, off-Broadway rock sound—even the Leo Sayer/Robin Williams rainbow suspenders sported by Reed on the inside cover. (I would have recommended that the producers replace the leather androgyne cartoon on the original cover with this photograph for the reissue.)

Instead, let's detail two material elements of the LP. As time has passed away and that old rock world no longer exists but in advertising, it would be a mistake to view this LP as a relic. In fact, I would go so far as to say that these historical elements diffuse the view; if you want to hear the real coked-out shit, I suggest you check out the collected works of Toto. As Reed says on the record, he does not need anybody to tell him he's good. However, writing in a comedy magazine as if I were a

Illustration by Jackie Gendel

rock critic, I do need to expound briefly upon two aspects of the album, primarily in order to demonstrate that I am smart, and also to recommend *Take No Prisoners*.

The first point is the binaural head technology used to record this live LP. Two sculpted human heads were placed in the venue at which *Take No Prisoners* was recorded; they functioned essentially as sound-wave filters that shaped the sound as it reached the microphones located in their ears. Each head produced a stereo signal to be specially mixed in an attempt to reproduce the actual process of human hearing. The head placement (one in the back of the venue and one near the stage) allows the mix to wander across the room as Reed and his band perform live, and it provides a musical equivalent to the shifts of focus that the performer undergoes as he works through his all-hit (at least to the audience at the time) repertoire.

Reed has stated that the binaural technology was not successful in this recording, but I find that the distortion and movement suits the material, removing it from the realm of plain document. A certain technological optimism is one of the elements of Reed's work that contributes to its richness—we're talking about a man whose favorite movie allegedly is *Tron*. By processing this live LP with binaural technology (an advanced concept of the time), the performance is immersed in a silicon-amber that preserves the instantaneously personal interaction of his 1978 shows behind a screen of electronic manipulation that allows the listener a level of detachment from the audience and the performer.

The second point is the material of the performance itself. Every day, then and now, two-bit electro-sonic wizards produce for our moronic desires a new technological miracle to remove the fabulous world of pop expression yet another realm beyond our reach. Many believe that replicas of the technology can bring a pure paradise where they can become replicas of pop expression itself. Inside this trauma, *Take No Prisoners* consummates music and comedy as a powerful and accessible conflict of energy and experience against worship and expectation. The word replaces the voice as an instrument inside the music; Reed expands the narrow allowances of comedy in rock and roll without resorting to the traduced standards of irony, pose or parody. On this LP, speech becomes freer than it has since become by rule and accepted practice as Reed pulls the potential of comedy into the conflicts that define rock and roll with a torrent of words driving the music, which in turn feeds the energy of the words. Where usually the mesmerizing power of a beat or sound carries with it the abstract power that causes the listener to feel something suggested by the music, here the word is used instead; but the ethical dilemmas of domination and control are resolved by the comedy, because the content of the sound is that of an individual confronting a mob. The word can have power over the listener, but it also exposes a vulnerability in the performer that cannot be hidden for the musical experience to succeed.

And succeed, at least commercially, *Take No Prisoners* did not. But take the LP to heart if you can cherish the thought of your own grace and grotesqueness in the same second and still feel beautiful. In light of the perennial "death of rock and roll" nonsense, I propose to you this overlooked possibility: funny as hell.

Lowbrow Reader #3, 2003

BANG + BOP COMICS

(an excerpt)

written by **JAY RUTTENBERG**   illustrated by **MIKE REDDY**

In 2003, I was assigned to interview the White Stripes for *Time Out New York*, where I was employed as a music critic. When asked where I wanted to meet the musicians, I suggested my cramped Manhattan apartment; for some reason, they agreed to this. What follows is an excerpt of "Bang & Bop," a comic book about the band's visit.—*JR*

Lowbrow Reader #5, 2006

FAT CHANCE, NEW MEXICO

by Neil Michael Hagerty

A T THE DOORS of the grocery store I was usually careful to look straight ahead, squinting a little, to avoid an
encounter with some poor meth head on probation shoving a
scrap of Jesus at me. They were forced, these addicts, to haunt
grocery store, street corner and taco truck; forced to hand out
pamphlets and sell candy. It was their bible-based community
service portion and the money went back to the church that
provided their substance-abuse treatment. This treatment was
chiefly composed of handing out pamphlets and selling candy,
and there was some praying involved, as well.

On the day this all started, I made the mistake of looking to
my right for oncoming cars as I crossed the parking lot, and I
had to refuse, quite stridently in fact, an offer to buy some Pixy
Stix. In my haste to escape, I bowled into the Gruber family as
they were leaving the store. Like many residents of this rural
bastion of illegible scorn and unremitting diabetes, the Grubers
were proudly cold to those outsiders who might be considered
comrades or equals, yet they were welcoming to those with bad
intentions. They greeted me warmly.

Gaylun, their teenage son, was restlessly herding them
through the throng around the popcorn machine, and he gave
me a frustrated look when they stopped to talk to me. The boy's
desperation was depressing to me, so I clapped Mr. Gruber on the

back, shot his wife a "finger gun" and kept moving into the store.

The next time I saw Gaylun Gruber, I was sitting at my desk before the most unfortunate view in the house. I was in front of a small window facing Zinc Street through a sickly bough of mesquite. My ex-girlfriend had exiled me to this room. I'd kept my desk here even after she'd vanished since the view afforded me no distraction. I could study the Gruber's back fence, the shed of the abandoned house behind them, and a flickering streetlight—or I could try to work.

It was around three in the morning and I was struggling to begin an article on Pixy Stix, the abrasive powder packaged in a plastic tube about the size of a drinking straw. Seeing them in the hands of the indentured meth addicts had led me to ponder some connection between drugs and childhood Pixy Stix indulgence. I thought it might be a bad idea to put clusters of these things into the unsupervised hands of addicts. When I was a kid, Pixy Stix came packaged in wax-coated paper straws, which was disappointing because the paper and powder invariably moistened, plugging the straw. Our solution to this was to slit them open with razor blades and dump them on a tabletop. We'd then collect the powder into piles and inhale three or four Stix in one gasp. The move to plastic straws addressed the clogging, not the practice of slitting. I knew also that Pixy Stix were made from D-glucose (dextrose monohydrate) and citric acid. Realizing with a shudder that I had very little to write about, I looked up to see Gaylun Gruber swinging down from his parents' fence into the yard of the abandoned house. A Latina girl about his age emerged from the shed and beckoned him inside. "Witness the failure of abstinence-only sex-ed," I remarked. "You have failed your final exam." Attending again to the notes on my desk, I confronted the dreary truth that the elegiac chiaroscuro portrait of Candy Land I had hoped to be creating would never be more than a dangling monochrome turd.

Night after night, Gaylun's conjugal visits to the shed continued. I wasn't much intrigued by it and I gave him his privacy, although his behavior remained amusing in one sense, given the Gruber family's typical racism. I dutifully pursued the Pixy Stix project, laboriously editing several pages of fluent spitting down to a few empty phrases. After a week of disinterest, the moment came when I was riveted to Gaylun's activities anew. I know for a fact it was around 3:48 in the morning because that's when the train comes through and the noise from the train made me stare out the window. Sound from a passing train reverberating through the flat desert streets keeps building. The shriek of the brakes, the horn, and the vibration of the long tracks are familiar immediately but the sound keeps coming for as long as it takes for the slowing train to pass through town. Stray sound starts to bounce back and pop out of time in relation to the work of the train. Is that a cat banging on the window with a timpani mallet? Is a woman sawing a fence post two blocks away? Is someone kicking a fence made of flattened oil pans? A low rumble is constant and you can feel it in your feet. It helps keep the mind from straying too far with imaginings, and eventually the train gets past the town, speeds up again, and the barking of dogs trails off. Then there's quiet and the pressure is gone.

As the train ran, I heard a car but saw no headlights. Then Gaylun appeared, coasting an old American rust bucket through the yard of the abandoned house, sidling it up to the doors of the shed. I was impressed that he'd waited to move the car under cover of the passing train.

Gaylun did not rush into the shed to see his girl this time, but instead left the doors of the car open and pulled a toolbox from the trunk. Leaning across the front seats, he started twisting and pounding with a variety of tools, occasionally emerging to set another injection-molded element on the grass. Having reassembled the entire dashboard beside the car, he began to clip and pull at the wiring, vents and frames inside the cavity, now exposed. Only after finishing this did he enter the shed. He and the girl returned to the car with piles of fat pillows that looked to be stuffed with extra weight. They set about positioning the pillows in the dashboard space using duct tape to hold them in place. Gaylun returned each piece of the dashboard to its interior position. He started the car. He executed a few slow turns, reverses and stops in the yard of the abandoned house. I

Illustration by Doreen Kirchner

noticed he avoided pumping the gas pedal too hard, careful not to make much noise. His girl gave him a wave and he cut the motor. They took the entire dashboard assembly apart, removed the pillows and replaced it again. Together, they pushed the car back onto the street, gave each other a farewell embrace and Gaylun drove away, alone.

So this, then, was the scheme for the two lovers, a drug-smuggling trip into nearby Mexico. A simple, lucrative drive across the border, its success all but assured by Gaylun's innocent looks and American passport. This sort of business was common, but it was usually confined to that segment of the population with roots in Mexico—at least, that's the story the arrest statistics told. After any drug bust, the reports in the local paper always stressed that the perpetrators were of a particular ethnicity and that they had relatively loose ties to the land here, being either recently arrived migrants or their criminally inclined children. It was commonly held that true citizenship was only granted to the second generation to be American-born, thus creating a weird competition between the cop and the priest to see who might capture the earliest genera-tion first and where their progeny might be anchored, whether in the prison or the maternity ward. There were also heard nefarious tales about how the drug cartels would hold random Mexicans hostage until their kin in the U.S.A. performed some sort of illegal task to secure their release. Perhaps this was the case with Gaylun's lover? Had she used her fecund wiles to entice him into this endeavor? The fact that she lived in a shed behind a vacant house suggested that she was anxious to keep herself hidden. Gaylun's lust, along with his birthright, must have made him appear to her a most appetizing rube.

Strolling along the downtown promenade, perusing the empty mall of empty buildings and payday loan outlets, I found my thoughts drifting back to Gaylun's earnest and enigmatic contrivances. Two days had passed since I witnessed the prepa-rations he and his lover had made for their outlaw adventure.

The future must seem a bright thing to the love struck. In passionate tumult was seen only the promise of wealth and liberty smuggling could bestow. I was coming to the conclusion that I would have to intervene in some way, to protect him, possibly, yes—but to humiliate the Grubers and their ilk, to expose the obliviousness that passed for political ideology. That was the real prize.

Fortune itself then goaded me into taking the first step in my plan, for it was at that very moment that I spied Gaylun's aunt, Doris, panting clumsily up the street toward me. Meeting her gaze, I politely stopped to wait for her to reach me in order to allow her plenty of room to decelerate. Doris was a single mother with a crafty soul; she was considered wise. She was envied by many in town, for it was believed that she had taken possession of the perfect boyfriend. She lived with a man who had received a serious head injury on his job at the electrical substation. Before the injury, he had been a well-developed and rugged physical specimen, and even after the blow to his head he remained so. The injury, however, had removed from his personality most traces of aggression except for a fierce and jealous loyalty to his new family. He did not have to leave for work and he desired no entertainment, so he was always available to watch the children and the property. Most important: Doris was the beneficiary of the man's workers' compensation money, a windfall made possible by the fact that the man had not one living relative.

Doris had finally pulled herself near to me. I could tell she had recently taken the local travel bath, a quick cleanse that involved wiping the pits and putting a little vanilla on the taint. It is suitable for shopping trips, attending city council meetings or conferring with undertakers after the death of a child. It is not suitable for church or church-related activities.

"Did you hear that another guy died at the emergency room? He was sitting there 14 hours before anyone noticed. That's four dead in a month. They're going to get sued out of business," Doris said.

"Drug poisoning again?" I asked. "Seems like everyone in town is worried about their family getting involved in the stuff. It's a panic."

"Oh, heck with that, everyone just better mind their business. We look after our own families, especially all the kids."

"Just sit them down for some straight talk about it, the drugs and the money for the drugs? That's the real problem, right, the easy money?"

"Well, it isn't a problem for my people. Maybe some others have to watch it, but in this family we make sure that no one needs to go outside the law for want of work or money. I've spoken to all my nieces and nephews about it and they know to steer clear of it or they'll have me to deal with."

We talked a while longer and I kept dodging the conversation away from the subject of drugs, crime and Gaylun, then returning ever closer to it in order to get her lay of the land. In the end, I was satisfied that she knew nothing of Gaylun's activities. As the shrewdest Gruber, she had tacitly confirmed to me that Gaylun had been careful to conceal his recent behavior from the clan. I said goodbye to Doris and she walked away, tilted forward slightly to use the stress of gravity to push her bulk onward. I watched as she heaved and lugged along her path until she disappeared around the corner.

I started thinking about the Venus of Willendorf and the kind of feckless fertility that decimates this town. While there are examples of fertility icons in Americana (and even icons of sterility worship), I wondered if there had ever been a kind of work or a function that was amusing or distracting enough to balance the power of the Venus with mockery but not with opposition; some ritual or some diversion ridiculing the worship of fertility in a lusty manner not based on suppression or the mechanics of sin.

The Venus of Willendorf, as you might recall from school, is that faceless and armless limestone statuette depicting a generously rounded female figure with swollen vulva and exaggerated breasts that dates from around 22 BCE. Since depictions of the human form are excluded from Upper Paleolithic art, it is generally accepted that the Venus is a depiction of fertility itself and, therefore, a ritual object of great power. It's not until the Neolithic era that we find some distinguishing remains of countervailing rituals among the nomadic tribes of the region. Carvings and other objects suggest a tradition of male figures mocking the fertility model, and perhaps even the presence of male artisans, rotund transvestite clowns, who performed distracting shamanistic rituals during fertility festivals. Among the Aztec, the spring ritual of Xipe Totec, our lord the flayed one, was led by a fat male priest wearing the flayed skin of a recently sacrificed human, an imitation of powerful fecundity. With the ancient Greeks, what we have come to call *comedy* was first spawned by self-mortifyingly bawdy phallic songs performed at fertility rituals by obese men. Later, among the *jongleurs*, the fat were considered the lewdest performers, while the *commedia* tradition had its chunky Dottor Balanzone.

In the Hopi Kachina Festival, a centuries-old fertility ceremony that continues to this day, the show begins with plump mud-smeared clowns invading the central plaza of the village. Working through the crowd, they perform variations of such recognizable clowning routines as: walking on air, crossbow drum, the young walk, the drunk walk, scarf juggling, feather balancing, mule parade and the naked truth. These antics are intended to distract celebrants away from the parade of painted Kachina dancers entering the square. This continues until the clowns meet the dancers at the center of the plaza and are tamed, cowed and drawn into the sacred space of the ritual, stripped of their burlesque powers.

In our America, the great corpulent men of comedy still carried on this ritual tradition. Technology and commercialization had made it all an empty reproduction parenthetical to its sacred roots, yet were not Fatty Arbuckle, John Belushi or Divine art-

ists in this vein? And maybe the reckless tragedy of the lives of
some of these comedians was due in part to the power associated
with assuming this ritual function in a modern society.

After a spell of research, I settled down to focus specifically
on the stout men of *MADtv*, the sketch comedy collaboration
between the Fox TV network and the humor magazine *MAD*.
In the 12 years the show has run, so far, there have been many
big men in the cast: Will Sasso, Artie Lange, Frank Caliendo,
Paul Vogt and, possibly, Bobby Lee and Aries Spears. By con-
necting the work and lives of these performers with the ancient
modes, I figured I could write a fairly substantial piece.

And so, I was back at my desk in the tiny room facing
Zinc Street. The piece was coming together, but I'd also found
myself restless to carry out the plan to get Gaylun Gruber
arrested. I guess I had assumed he'd do the deed within a few
days since he'd already tested out the hiding place for the drugs,
but here it was one week since I'd watched them take the car
apart. He'd hit the shed once or twice, but the launch-time for
the big project never seemed to come. Gradually, I'd become
bogged down with my writing, too. It was easy enough to go
on about the ancient stuff and even to connect it to some of the
practices of the modern day and the specific roles of the *MADtv*
fat men, but I needed that insider perspective to really bring
the piece alive. Interviews with some of the performers would
give it a depth that could take it beyond mere social conjecture
into the realm of something someone could actually give a shit
about. But when I thought of talking about this stuff with a
professional comedian I started to feel like an idiot. I mean, the
pomposity of the writing in relation to the subject was funny,
but bringing that nonsense to one of these guys would just be
retarded. Maybe I'd get someone else to do the interviews as
cover, or maybe I could grab quotes out of old interviews. I was
stuck.

But as the saying goes around here, the Lord will provide,
and just then Gaylun Gruber pulled the car into the lot of the

Illustration by Doreen Kirchner

abandoned house once again. The girl emerged from the shed furtively, climbed in and they were out of there. Go time had finally arrived. I moved away from the window, crouching down until I was certain they were gone. I gave them 30 minutes to get past the border and then I went to the gas station and called the sheriff, the DEA tip line, Crimestoppers, Border Patrol and State Police. Disguising my voice, I gave them the plate number, a description of the car and its passengers and said they'd be carrying a huge stash back from Mexico.

I saw no word of the bust in the newspaper as I ate my lunch at the taco truck the following day. It wasn't totally surprising— stories leaked out sometimes weeks after they had occurred, since the paper here was just another wing of the Chamber of Commerce. I'd thought that maybe the sensational elements of the story might have encouraged them to run it right away, as a morality tale for the kids, but I wasn't shocked at the silence.

Then I heard two old ladies in the lunch crowd gossiping while they waited to be served.

"Ray said they got caught coming in last night on the U.S. side. They got an anonymous tip, he said, and—"

"Who was it called them?"

"They don't know—just a deep voice, big and scary sounding. The sheriff on duty called Ray first thing and they went down there. Well, sure enough, there's the car that matches the description, flew right through the Mexican side—but our guys stopped it and pulled it apart. He said the kids were crying and pleading that they didn't know anything about drugs and that Gaylun was just bringing his fiancée back from visiting her family. But they brought the dogs in and went ahead and checked the trunk, the tires and all. The dogs got a hit inside the car so they pulled the dashboard apart and that's when they found the two women stuffed inside.

It turns out it was the girl's mother and sister from Mexico. Gaylun was bringing them across as illegals. Ray sat in on the questioning and it came out that Gaylun was bringing them in so that he and the girl could have a proper wedding since they're in love, but she's Catholic and wouldn't do it without having her mother and sister stay with her. That was their plan, but it's all put an end to now. The girl is getting deported. The way Ray tells it, Gaylun is really in trouble. He has to face charges of human smuggling, and no getting around it. It's a terrible thing for the Gruber family, I have to say, it's really a shame."

Lowbrow Reader #6, 2008

In 1996, soon after Muhammad Ali lit the torch to launch Atlanta's Olympic games, the boxer met with novelist Gilbert Rogin in New York City. Rogin—a former Sports Illustrated *editor who covered Ali early in both men's careers—wrote the following account. It remained untouched until the summer of 2009 when Rogin, just shy of 80, read the article at Soho's Housing Works Bookstore Café as part of the Lowbrow Reader Variety Hour. He shared the bill with the Fiery Furnaces, John Mulaney, Larkin Grimm and Peter Stampfel's Ether Frolic Mob.*

ME AND ALI
by *Gilbert Rogin*

SERIOUSLY, FOLKS

Sitting on a couch in a midtown Manhattan hotel suite, the Champ seems to have fallen asleep, just like that, chin on chest, eyes shut. Now he's snoring big-time.

Seriously, folks....

Lonnie Ali, the Champ's wife, says, "Muhammad's very comfortable with himself, isn't he? Now he has a condition. He has flashbacks. Some form of narcolepsy."

As if on cue, the Champ begins throwing baby hooks in his sleep.

Suddenly he erupts, roaring, lunging at me like a spectral contrivance in the Tunnel of Love. "He was faking it!" I shriek.

"He's always faking it, isn't he?" Lonnie says.

"He hasn't changed," I say.

"Still a baby," Lonnie says, "still spoiled, still rotten."

Seriously, folks, this is Muhammad Ali, at 56 conceivably the world's preeminent humanitarian, who last year was honored by, among others, Amnesty International, with its Lifetime Achievement Award, and by the UN as its Messenger of Peace.

COMMERCIAL BREAK

The Champ is available for card shows and has a very attractive line of ties and boxer shorts.

THE SMILE

The Champ may also be the world's most famous person.

"Did you know that?" I ask him.

"Try not to think about it because it'll make your head big," he says.

I say, "You got a big head anyway. Look at the size of it."

Getting back at him for scaring the shit out of me.

The Champ smiles. Unlike most people, who narrow their eyes when they smile, the Champ opens his wide, almost popping them, and his cheeks swell wonderfully and somehow take on a rosy glow, as if a bulb had lit up inside his mouth.

HIS SENSE OF HUMOR

"What did Abraham Lincoln say after a two-day binge?"

"O.K., what?"

"'Free *who*?'"

Lonnie says, "Muhammad's never been politically correct. And he never will be."

"'Free the *who*,'" the Champ says, cracking himself up.

No way I'm going to tell you the one about the Jews and the canoes.

BACK IN THE DAY

I've known the Champ since 1961. I looked it up. Unlike most of us, he's had the kind of life you can look up. Feb. 7, 1961, Slim Jim Robinson, Miami Beach, TKO 1. Then, of course, he was Cassius Clay. Some of us couldn't make the transition, so Champ is what we call him, which he was, is, forever will be.

At first, he was up on his toes, hands by his sides, big man dancing, nobody touching him. He simply wasn't there as, in Atlanta, so many years later, he was suddenly, omnipotently there, entrusted with the torch, fulfilling our unrealized longing.

Then he was flat-footed, taking shots. Then he wasn't coming out of his corner for the 12th round. Oct. 2, 1980, Larry Holmes, Las Vegas, TKO by 11. Then he got Parkinson's. Lonnie (wife No. 4 who bore him child No. 9) lived across the street from him in Louisville and had worshipped him since she was 6. "And then she grew up," the Champ was saying, marveling. And he drew an hourglass in the air. "Except now he likes blondes," Lonnie said.

THE LOW FIVE

The Champ makes to give me a low five. I extend my hand, palm up. He swats and misses. At first, I feel sorry for him. Upon reflection, I realize the Champ didn't make contact because my hand was in the wrong place. I move it an inch to the left. *Awwright!*

THE KISS

"We've taken up enough of your time," I say, getting up.

The Champ applauds. *Chochem.* Then he says, "Did you get a good interview?" Sweet man.

When I get to the door, for some reason I turn and look back. That's what we're doing nowadays, the Champ and I, looking

Illustration by Jackie Gendel

back, seeking a lot of things, finding a few, I guess. Whatever, the Champ is standing in the middle distance. He gently raises his right hand to his lips, blows me a kiss.

When Ali materialized in Atlanta, lit the Olympic flame, it's safe to say he moved the world, many to tears. For my part, I smiled—and exhaled. I was so proud of him. He was so still, serene, dignified. And he didn't drop the fucking thing!

I've written so much about the Champ that sometimes I think I've made him up, if you know what I'm saying. Can't make *this* up: When Ali softly blew me that kiss, his hand moving so slowly over so short a distance from his mouth to where he let it flutter and gently fall, I started to cry at last. Got me again.

Lowbrow Reader #8, 2010

LETTER FROM THE EDITOR: ON JOURNALISM

by Jay Ruttenberg

Hey Edit Staffers,

You don't need me to tell you about the state of our industry. To give a précis, our newspaper's print circulation currently extends to writers of ransom notes; a cruel man on Oak Street who uses the publication to whack his dog; and stubborn, elderly shut-ins who refuse to get with the times and will likely die soon—say next year, when the city's 911 emergency number moves online. Finances remain tight: Many of you have already enjoyed the Subway subs franchise we are leasing from the space that the Xerox machines, now pawned, formerly occupied. And if our predictions for the next fiscal quarter prove accurate, and advertising drops 260 percent, things are likely to get worse still.

Conversely, our online readership has hit an all-time high. The union may have balked at our added web responsibilities, but I think we can all agree that writing five to six blog posts per day is a more gratifying activity than waiting on a bread line. I take particular pride in specialty blogs like the Thongista, in which Doug posts images of underwear advertisements for those teenage readers who once turned to the print edition for such material, and Rotten Fish Wrap, in which we write about how horrible newspapers are.

And so, our company has reached a crucial turning point. Either we stick with the old model and sink, like all those squeaky-voiced silent movie stars at the dawn of talkies, or we adapt to the world's technological challenges and stay afloat, like pushy industrialists elbowing their way onto the *Titanic's* lifeboats. Some of these changes are simple, such as providing a web link for every noun appearing in the newspaper, or creating a Facebook group for each front-page article. Others may seem more complex, especially to those older staffers who have yet to accept our buy-out package of JC Penney coupon books and frozen hamburger meat. But I trust that both of you will quickly immerse yourselves in the exciting world of widgets, tumblelogs, Skype chats with angry letter-writers, inserting your columns into online video games, editing Wikipedia entries to reflect your reporting, hacking Digg, recording podcasts for the benefit of readers who do not like to read, and writing headlines found vivid and engaging by Google's search engine.

Let's look at two articles, both covering local fires. The first was written by a former staff reporter and current short-order cook. "A ferocious inferno swept through a four-story building on Main Street early Friday morning," it begins. The article goes on to quote the building owner and distressed neighbors; I'm sure my grandfather would have found it riveting. Now, let's see Doug's piece, filed after a warehouse blaze last week. He dispensed with a traditional lede, instead live-blogging the event and sending Twitter tweets with all the basic information. A YouTube video showed Doug chatting with local hipsters about the neighborhood's loft scene, while an iMeem stream allowed people to enjoy a selection of pop tunes—"Burning Down the House," "Hot in Herre" and the like—while they read. Working in conjunction with scientists at the university, Doug developed primitive scratch-and-sniff Internet technology allowing readers to experience what fire smells like. Finally, Doug provided a link of his piece to bitchybitchygaymedia.com so that the website's commentators could ridicule the moustache of one of the

Illustration by Mike Reddy

firefighters, who tragically died. All this from an intern!

These are the reporting skills we all must develop if we are to stay off welfare in the 21st century. Sure, there have been bumps along the road. Like when, in lieu of a traditional article about the gubernatorial election, we linked to a rival paper, not knowing that their article merely provided a link to our own story. Or when Huan, the correspondent from Tuvalu to whom we outsourced the Hollywood beat, mistook Angelina Jolie for a primeval serpentine goddess, returning to earth to raise holy hell in time for the apocalypse. Or when we learned that Huan had outsourced his responsibilities to an elderly woman in the Republic of Namibia. Or when Doug mispronounced Mayor Muthirfucir's name in his hourly video blog, and all of the staffers experienced enough to catch the error were in a seminar about RSS Feeds.

Or when we attempted to oust Terry as the paper's film critic in favor of a commentator who had wittily flamed him on a discussion board, and then discovered that the commentator was in fact Terry himself, desperately trying to stir up web attention. Or the incident with the Bengal tiger. Or when we promised cash bonuses to the writers of the paper's three most e-mailed articles, and all three spots were occupied by sugar-cookie recipes from the syndicated column "Baking Healthy with Dr. Laurie." Or when we couldn't afford to pay our web server, and the penis-enlargement site that squatted on our domain won a Pulitzer Prize for public service. And yes, spelling errors have proliferated since we replaced the copy department with Lincoln Elementary School's fifth grade English class—but from what Mrs. O'Malley tells me, the incoming fourth graders are a much sharper lot.

Now for the love of Christ, get tweeting, journalists!

Lowbrow Reader #7, 2009

HEY, JAZZMAN, IS THAT A PIE IN YOUR GUITAR?

Slim Gaillard and the Flat Foot Floogie

by Michaelangelo Matos

MUSICIANS MAY SING for their supper, but the ones that I like best tend to be those who sing *about* it. Aside from love and sex, food is pop music's, if not the world's, great universal subject, and food songs tend to be pretty reliable indicators that the person doing the singing doesn't take what they do too seriously. Love and sex may be silly, but too often people sing about them like they're the end of the goddamn world or something. Not so songs about eats: Even instrumentals named after dishes tend to indicate a sprier worldview than most. Would Dead Can Dance or Nine Inch Nails perform numbers such as "Pass the Peas" or "Fried Neck Bones and Some Homefries"? I rest my cakes.

Bulee "Slim" Gaillard (who was born in either 1911 or 1916 and most definitely died in 1991) didn't sing about food exclusively. But he explored the subject frequently enough to clue listeners into his essential impishness, and that's before we even get to the nonsense numbers and genre parodies. Gaillard was best known as a guitarist, and on that instrument he was sly, sneaky, droll; so was his singing, especially as he got older. But he played several instruments well, and on a few early '50s numbers, he even overdubbed himself into a full band—an especially unusual practice during the era, Les Paul notwithstanding. As a musician, Gaillard commanded enough respect to perform with

Charlie Parker and Dizzy Gillespie around the time they were changing the face of jazz in the mid-'40s. (They were, naturally, his sidemen.)

I know Gaillard's work primarily through three compilation CDs. Slim & Slam's *The Groove Special* features 1938–1942 material recorded with and without early bassist and co-vocalist Leroy "Slam" Stewart. It's got Gaillard's signature tunes, "The Flat Foot Floogie" ("And a floy-floy / Flow-joy, flow-joy, flow-joy"—the original title was "Floozie," which makes you wonder just what kind of joy was flowing) and "Groove Juice Special" (featuring a tap-dance solo by Slim), and it's manic and eager to please. *An Introduction to Slim Gaillard: His Best Recordings 1938–1946* is a harder-to-find collection on the French label Best of Jazz that emphasizes Slim the musician over Slim the joker, and features three of the Parker/Gillespie numbers, the best of which is the sublimely loose-limbed "Slim's Jam." *Laughing in Rhythm: The Best of the Verve Years*, which covers 1946–1954, is the flat-out funniest of the three, courtesy of the title song (chorus: "Ah-ha-ha-ha-ha-ha / Ah-ha-ha-ha-ha-ha") and the ridiculous "Serenade to a Poodle," likely the silliest music he ever recorded.

This is saying something, because Gaillard's personal lexicon took hepcat jive into the outer limits. His penchant for affixing "vout" or "orooney" or their even more onomatopoeic progeny ("Vout Oreenee" is the name of a 1945 song on *An Introduction*) to every available noun became his trademark. When introduced to Mickey Rooney, Gaillard asked him, in all apparent seriousness, what his last name was. On "Slim's Jam," Gaillard introduces tenor saxist Jack McVea as "Jack McVoutee," Parker is transformed into "Charlie Yardbird-Orooney," and Gillespie becomes "Daz McSkivven Vouts-Orooney"; after their solos, Gaillard instructs them to fetch him a double order of reetie-voutie with hot sauce, an orange soda and "a big bowl of avocado seed soup while we nail the seeds to the roof, and that'll fix it," respectively.

Gaillard might have treated English like a foreign language, but that was nothing compared to how he treated actual foreign languages and dialects. These were a major fascination of his, one he said came from his father's work as a ship steward. (Allegedly, the elder Gaillard mistakenly left his son in Crete for six months, where young Slim picked up Greek; Slim claimed to have learned half a dozen languages from his travels with his father.) Needless to say, he wasn't any more reverent with other tongues than with his own. Slim & Slam's treatment of "Chinatown, My Chinatown" is gonzo bordering on racist, the

Slim Gaillard meeting Mickey Rooney / Illustration by Doreen Kirchner

222 | THE LOWBROW READER READER

two vocalists erupting into demented cod-Chinese nonsense-speak on the bridge and final chorus. "Matzoh Balls" is sung, for some reason, in apparent homage to Jimmy Durante. His Yma Sumac impersonation is preserved on the nutso "Soony Roony (Song of Yxabat)," in which Slim flips between sounding like Peter Lorre and a maniacal parakeet.

But as noted, nothing got Slim going like food. The refrain of "Potato Chips" puts years of Pringles advertising to shame: "Crunch, crunch, I don't want no lunch / All I want is potato chips." "Tutti Frutti" abjures vanilla and chocolate, though he allows that "strawberry will do." (The title isn't the only thing that makes one wonder how big a Gaillard fan Richard Penniman was when he was Little.) "Chicken Rhythm" approximates live clucking but hints at meals to come, while "Matzoh Balls" also honors gefilte fish. The title of "Yep Roc Heresy," a non-food song, was swiped from a Syrian restaurant menu; "Serenade to a Poodle" hits its moment of transcendence during the bridge, when Gaillard belts, "Hamburger! Cheeseburger! Hamburger! *Boneburger!*"

At the end of the '50s, an exhausted Gaillard stopped touring. "I was eating one, missing 10," he told reporter Mike Zwerin. "I'd start a hamburger today and finish it the day after tomorrow." (Gaillard's comments about boneburgers remain unreported.) Settling in Los Angeles, where he was still a nightclub draw, he shifted into character acting before buying a fruit orchard near Tacoma, Washington. By the early '80s, with encouragement from his old friend Dizzy Gillespie, Gaillard was playing European jazz festivals; he was an especially popular draw in England, and he remained so until 1991, when he died of cancer.

Lowbrow Reader #2, 2002

A SURVEY OF
DECLASSIFIED LITERATURE
by Neil Michael Hagerty

T*ear the Lid Offa that Sucker: Notes from the Font* reprints a
selected history of the *Quizzler* magazine, published and
masterminded by the unflappable Biggie Banks. In its heyday,
the now-defunct *Quizzler* sought to educate the complacent
college graduate while arousing him to a revolutionary rub by
singling out local and federal heresy or, alternately, by following Mr. Banks's handful of friends as they "ironically" moved
through the capital markets in various family-funded profes-
sions. In the simplest possible language (with a liberal splash of
exclamation points), the *Quizzler* detailed the method by which
certain presumably banal phenomena related to the vague feeling many of us hold that "everything is a load of horseshit."

Highlights include: An exegesis on the nine-digit zip-code
system that clearly explains how we are all numbered, observed,
and visited by a shadowy government agency known cryptically
as the "Post Office."

A terse but scathing indictment of Wonder Bread that
simply lists the ingredients of the bread in a larger, more eru-
dite typeface that makes clear the implications of such other-
worldly concepts as "phosphate-bilex-12" and "retardant" without offending the elevated taste of the common readership.

A biographical sketch of Mr. Banks's college roommate,
the well-known grist pimp Pendelton LeSard Walker, as he

bemusedly grins his way through the vain, high-stakes world of rubber-stamp collecting.

The now-legendary "Superman Is Not a Real Person."

....

Joan Davis's new one is called *Turd Burglar*. As many of us feared after last year's PEN Awards set-to, Ms. Davis has become obsessed by what she likes to call "the exceptional use of whiskey to make words float through the air with dignity and land upon the ear with an endorsed weight." Physical conceits aside, I found this volume largely readable. In one particularly fine essay, Ms. Davis analyzes the subversive misuse of trans-literation in the national news media by discussing the various pronunciations of "Taliban" (including, though by no means limited to, "Tuh-Lee-Bin," "Tally-Bahn," "Tully-Bin," "Tallow-Bun," and "Los-An-Juh-Lees").

....

Next on this tearstained list, I must note Percy Schlimazel's *An Unfinished Treatise on an Incomplete Shit.*

The golden triangle of "Mind, Body and Soul," which has been adapted and revered from the High Greeks through to our own Presidential Fitness Awards, seems to have given way in modern culture to the Sunday Triangle of "Football, Beer and Sex." Yet upon closer examination, we find that only the names have changed, and the balance of human spirit remains strong. *Football* corresponds to *Mind, Beer* to *Body*, and *Sex* to *Soul*. The Golden Triangle is still the basis for our culture and an unassailable target for racists (unlike the Triangle Offense).

In keeping with the well-known theory of the Western Canon, in which powerful literature flourishes best beneath the shielding vaults of the powerful, Mr. Schlimazel has selected the Western Cannon (a.k.a. Rich Gannon, a.k.a. "The Gray Cannon,"

Well-known grist pimp Pendelton LeSard Walker / Illustration by Carl Cassel

QB for the Oakland Raiders at age 36) to represent the powerful central figure of poise and clarity, whose statistics, biogra-
phy and performance can shield adherents to the New Golden
Triangle against the class-ridden denigrators of the modern
philosophy (a.k.a. bosses, wives, cocktail party know-it-alls).

Mr. Schlimazel's new work presents the tale of Solomon
Peters as he enters into adolescence at the astonishing age of
33. When we meet him, Solomon has fallen in with a gang of
dandies, with whom he roams the beaches of San Diego. By day,
they smoke glue through bongs filled with Mountain Dew and
terrorize sunbathers by pulling their hair and running away;
by night, they crowd the Karaoke Bars of Ocean Beach, entering contests for chump change. It is here that Solomon finds
himself onstage during David Allan Coe Night. At a crucial
point in the contest, just as he is about to advance to the finals,
Solomon freezes and can only manage to murmur the Loggins
and Messina song "House at Pooh Corner." Humiliated, he
shaves his wig and then removes it. Later, after having won by
knockout the love of a good woman, Solomon retreats with her
into the arcane of the Kabbalah. At first, he is not sure if she is
a Theosophic fascist or just really Jewish, but faith wins out.

In order to perfect himself for his beloved, he secretly plans
to convert religions. Solomon undergoes an operation to reat-
tach his foreskin. Although this adds almost two inches to his
penis size, it does not impress the parents of his girlfriend, and
they beseech him to attend the required religious classes or, bar-
ring time constraints, forge some genealogy.

The well-faked climax of the novel reveals Solomon rising
from the confusing mire of his search for meaning through an
epiphany achieved one Sunday in November as he simultaneously receives oral sex and chugs a beerbong as, on TV, Rich
Gannon delivers a perfectly placed pass into the outstretched
arms of Tim Brown in the back of the endzone. Time appears to
stop, or perhaps run backward (this is not made entirely clear),
as an apparition of the Western Cannon himself emerges from

the TV screen and sits Solomon down to deliver "The Holy Playbook" word-by-word. Although this enforced reference to the Mahabharata is amusing, if not altogether transparent, the novel ends before the Word is fully revealed. Hopefully, Mr. Schlimazel will write quickly and get the third and final book

Solomon onstage during David Allan Coe Night / Illustration by Carl Cassel

in this trilogy out before autumn. I hate when they leave you hanging just when things get interesting. When will I learn?

....

Finally, we have Bruno Foro's *Lo Stronzo dell' Ufficio Affianco* (The Asshole in the Next Cubicle), published in a new translation by Kenyon DeLawter, Assistant State Poet of Arkansas. Despite its 2001 copyright, this pastiche of morbidity seems unduly timely, for we now see the effects of our epic transition from a vigorous nation of thieves into a passive-aggressive troupe of clowns waiting under the sewer grate to collect the various bits of loose change that the big dogs let fall from their pockets along with lint, condom wrappers and half-chewed mints. Mr. Foro axes us all: "What is the deal?"

Unlike many *elite-istas* who seem to feel that pointing out obvious incidents of cowardice or venality amounts to circumscribing some wider-ranging set of social injustices, Mr. Foro gives the reader a set of possible choices to act upon, if one were so inclined on such a lovely Sunday as this. For example, the old "lock the boss out of his own office" routine has been clearly notated in simple step-by-step instructions worthy of Bob Vila. The gimmick here is to remove the hinges, drop the deadbolt on

Illustration by Carl Cassel

the inside, swing the door shut using the reinserted deadbolt as a hinge, and so forth.

I must add one basic caveat to this review. As I do not understand *una sola parola d' italiano,* I am not entirely sure that this book is not, in fact, a collection of Dilbert-like musings on the perplexities of life in the information-technology sector (with a spicy Roman twist). Some research has come across my desk that suggests DeLawter, the translator, has been embroiled in an interoffice feud with his boss (the State Poet-in-Chief of Arkansas) and may have injected some personal venom into this otherwise un-besmirched translation. I will leave interpretation to the reader, however, because like all great works of art, *Lo Stronzo dell' Ufficio Affianco* draws much of its strength from subtle ambiguity, and it is profusely illustrated.

Lowbrow Reader #2, 2002

OVERLOOKED COMEDIES:
1961-1983

by Sam Henderson
Illustrations by Alex Eben Meyer

PEOPLE WHO KNOW me consider me a "humor snob." Much of my own work in comics has been about dissecting various conventions in comedy. This can be funny for a print audience, but somewhat off-putting when watching a movie or TV show with me and hearing me constantly say, "That scene would be funnier if...."

But no matter how much I complain later, I'll still watch almost anything that's supposed to be funny. A friend of mine teaches film to students who constantly ask him why he hates everything—to which he replies, "I love more films than you've ever seen!" I guess that's how I am when it comes to comedy. Humor has always been the bastard genre of any medium, and accordingly some examples are rarely mentioned, even by comedy geeks.

This is not a best or worst list—in fact, it's pretty random. It's not a list of all-time favorites, as most of those have had more than enough coverage. Some here are unfairly overlooked, some justifiably. Many are shown on cable quite frequently and others are available at any Blockbuster. I know that when I'm finished writing, I'll come up with dozens more that could have been used.

ONE, TWO, THREE (1961)
KISS ME, STUPID (1964)

Billy Wilder was often known for being topical. Topical plus time sometimes equals dated, which may be why these two films are rarely mentioned in Wilder's oeuvre. *One, Two, Three* was shot in Berlin while the Wall was being built, in anticipation of the imminent split. James Cagney, in his next-to-last film role, plays MacNamara, a Coca-Cola executive recently transferred to Germany who has to remind his new employees that they no longer need to goosestep. His loyalty to his job and "language lessons" from his secretary Ingeborg (Liselotte Pulver) constantly put his family life in jeopardy. On top of this, he has now agreed to host his boss's teenage daughter Scarlett (Pamela Tiffin) during her stay in Germany.

Scarlett sneaks out of the house and parties every night; later, she confesses to marrying young communist Otto Piffl (Horst Buchholz), oblivious to the consequences. (She thinks "Yankee Go Home" is an American North/South sentiment rather than a West/East German one.) In addition to his other problems, MacNamara now also has to negotiate with the East Germans before his boss flies in—either to have the marriage annulled or to get Western citizenship for Otto. In one scene, he uses Ingeborg to seduce them at a club, and they bang their shoes on the table, causing the picture of Khrushchev to fall off the wall and reveal a picture of Stalin underneath. Such specific references are probably a reason *One, Two, Three* hasn't endured as well as other Cold War comedies like *Dr. Strangelove*.

Kiss Me, Stupid is similar in that the main character is conflicted between saving his marriage and promoting his career; ultimately, he does both through a series of complicated schemes. Orville Spooner (Ray Walston) is a piano teacher in Climax, Nevada, who, together with the neighboring gas-station attendant, Barney (Cliff Osmond), dreams of hitting it big as a songwriter. When Dean Martin (who more or less plays himself) breaks down while driving through town, Barney seizes the opportunity. He claims that the repairs will take a while, so Dino will have to stay in town overnight. The hope is that Dino will hear their songs when he stays with the Spooners and like them so much he'll buy them.

Though Wilder's films always broke taboos—and there was never any question that they were for adults—*Kiss Me, Stupid* was considered *too* adult. There's nothing here that couldn't be shown in a prime-time sitcom today, but the themes and dialogue were too much for audiences and critics at the time—particularly the conclusion, which seems daring by any era's standards.

HOW TO MURDER YOUR WIFE (1965)
LORD LOVE A DUCK (1966)

The late playwright George Axelrod (*The Seven Year Itch*, *The Manchurian Candidate*) had a successful stage-to-screen track record, and eventually wrote for film directly, sometimes helming the director's chair. The quality of his output varied, but his best writing was on a par with any of his contemporaries.

As a cartoonist, I can vouch for the accuracy in which the profession is portrayed in *How to Murder Your Wife*. Bachelor Stanley Ford (Jack Lemmon) has his own townhouse, maintained with the aid of his manservant Charles (Terry-Thomas). His daily syndicated "Bash Brannigan" is wildly popular, its realism due to his living each adventure before drawing it. After one night of drunken revelry, he wakes up to find he has married an Italian stripper (Virna Lisi). He tries to make the best of it, though it prevents him from hanging out with his cronies, and makes Charles feel obsolete. More importantly, his marriage has compromised his strip, which has evolved from Steve Canyon–like gritty adventure into a domestic comedy à la Blondie. The only solution to these conflicts of interest is alluded to in the title; he gets busted, naturally, when the situation is paralleled

Lord Love a Duck

Oh Dad, Poor Dad

in the comic. (Those expecting a literal step-by-step guide will be disappointed.)

Lord Love a Duck is something like *Rushmore* or *Heathers* re-written by Terry Southern. Roddy McDowall (nearly 40 at the time the movie was filmed) plays high-school psycho Alan "Mollymauk" Musgrave, who finds a kindred spirit in vulnerable new student Barbara Ann Greene (Tuesday Weld), who lives with her negligent mother (Lola Albright) and longs to be a star. He expresses his love by making all her wishes come true by whatever means necessary. In turn, she learns how to manipulatively use her feminine charms, whether on her school principal (Harvey Korman) or when shopping with her father (Max Showalter, in one of the most creepily erotic scenes this side of Nabokov).

Each time you think Alan's behavior can't get more relentless, he further surprises you. After Barbara drops out and marries Billy (David Draper), she confesses her unhappiness to Alan, who unsuccessfully tries to murder him several times. Each attempt becomes increasingly severe and blatant—poisoning, brake-tampering, and eventually trying to run Billy over while a huge crowd looks on—yet Billy has no clue that Alan has it in for him.

Viewers will notice the presence of boom mikes a few times in the frame—I think this may be intentional if it's not a 35-to-16-mm flub. Although it was his directorial debut, Axelrod was enough of a veteran to have had higher production values if he had so wanted. Since some of the conventions of drive-in features of the time are parodied, it's likely he was trying to make the whole movie look like one.

YOU'RE A BIG BOY NOW (1966)
THE KNACK...AND HOW TO GET IT (1965)
OH DAD, POOR DAD... (1967)

A recurring premise in comedies for a while was the lonely, introspective young man coming into adulthood. He's usually behind his peers in sexual experience; either unsuccessfully trying to get laid, or only now discovering that the opportunity exists. The few friends he has don't get his eccentricities. He still has a thin strand of umbilical cord left—his interaction with his parents often explains a lot. *The Graduate* and *Harold and Maude,* to different extents, are the two most famous examples.

One early entry in the "1960s blue-balled man-child" genre was written and directed by Francis Ford Coppola. *You're a Big Boy Now* depicts the life of 19-year-old Bernard Chanticleer (Peter Kastner), living in New York for the first time. Even though he's paying rent in his own apartment, his parents (Rip Torn and Geraldine Page) still hold tight reins from upstate. He works at the New York Public Library under his father, and his mother imposes heavy restrictions enforced by his landlady, Miss Thing (Julie Harris).

Bernard's daydreaming and clumsiness constantly get him into hot water at work. Presumably, he has this job because he can't keep one anywhere else, since his father obviously has more faith in Bernard's cohort Raef (Tony Bill). The Raef character is common in these kinds of movies—the friend who always scores with women, and will show you how he does it as long as he has first pick. Bernard wants Barbara Darling (Elizabeth Hartman), an aloof theater seamstress. They're the same age, but the fact that he's lived half his and she twice hers makes her even less accessible. He has a sure thing with co-worker Amy (Karen Black), but his infatuation with Barbara blows it. When he does deign to date Amy and tries to bring her home, it scares Miss Thing's pet chicken, which is there to prevent him from bringing women home in the first place.

An extra bonus is that everything is filmed on location, providing a glimpse of New York City as it looked in 1965. We see candid footage of Times Square, its porn theaters, underground clubs, department stores, and probably the only record of the NYPL's pneumatic retrieval system. The film's fast pacing and free-spirited mood are similar to the style that expatriate Richard Lester was developing across the ocean.

The Knack...and How to Get It is similar to *Big Boy* in many ways, particularly with the theme of the naïf/cad/girl triangle. It's also shot entirely on location: This time, the backdrop is swinging London. The film opens with a pan showing a long line of birds waiting to shag Tolen (Ray Brooks), which frustrates flatmate Colin (Michael Crawford) to no end. In a fit of sympathy, Tolen takes Colin under his wing and teaches him how to get "The Knack," but inevitably the new girl in town comes between them. Colin is genuinely smitten by Nancy (Rita Tushingham) while Tolen wants her mostly because he can get her.

Director Richard Lester continues in the proto-music video vein he developed previously with *A Hard Day's Night.* There's a lot of improvisation not only in the acting, but in the direction as well. When the guys buy a king-size bed and cart it back home, meeting Nancy along the way, it's evident that Lester and crew chose locations on the spot, creating the final product through editing. There are several great gags in the apartment based on recurring obstacles, like the new bed forever stuck sideways in the stairwell, and third roommate Tom (Donal Donnelly) obsessively house painting.

Tolen runs away with Nancy and Colin plays the hero, which

leads to a bizarre moment in which Nancy, believing they have conspired to rape her, runs through the streets yelling accusations. I'm not sure if the ensuing montage is meant to be funny in this case, as Lester's trademark rapid-fire cuts go by of Nancy shouting "Rape!" to random people and objects, with varying inflections. It seems to have been common to make light of rape in the '60s and '70s the same way blackface was acceptable in the early 20th century. I guess I'll rationalize it that way.

Arthur Kopit's Off Broadway play, *Oh Dad, Poor Dad, Mama's Hung You in the Closet and I'm Feelin' So Sad*, was the story of virginal Jonathan Rosepettle, forced to travel around with his widowed mother and stay indoors—with his father's corpse—while she's out all day crusading against sin. He's not supposed to talk to anyone, especially not the tramp next door, whom he has no idea is coming on to him, anyway. It all takes place in the hotel room and there are rarely ever more than two people present, which is not unusual for a play. Moviegoers, however, may feel cheated sitting through a film in which much of the backstory is revealed through dialogue and seen through one camera. It could have been jazzed up a little.

Establishing shots and extra cameras are a start, but not always enough. A catchy theme song by the Neal Hefti Singers would help. More mugging, and a chase scene toward the end. Rosalind Russell and Robert Morse are big draws, Richard Quine is a relatively competent director, but something's still missing. How about editing Jonathan Winters in at the last minute? Make him the dead father who prefaces the story up in heaven, explaining how glad he is to be rid of his family and why. During the slow parts, stop the action and put Winters in a corner box to belittle his son and wife with one-liners! Perfect!

The play was not meant to be "funny" in the same way the movie was executed. My guess is that the movie rights were bought to cash in on the long titles some comedies had in the '60s. The film is as overly long as the title, and I only recommend it to those with a very high tolerance for such humor.

THE LOVE GOD? (1969)
I LOVE YOU, ALICE B. TOKLAS! (1968)

How do you satirize the sexual revolution and keep a G-rating? Six words: Don Knotts is...*The Love God?* Wholesome funnyman Knotts is cast as Abner Peacock in this tale written and directed by Nat Hiken (*Sgt. Bilko, Car 54*—the original TV versions, not the lame movie remakes). Abner is publisher of *Peacock's Quarterly*, a bird-watchers' magazine that has been in his family for generations. On the verge of bankruptcy, last-minute investor Osborn Tremaine (Edmond O'Brien) comes through and takes editorial control while Abner is on an expedition. Abner doesn't find out until it's too late that he's the fall guy for this new investor: a convicted pornographer who is using the magazine as a front for smut. Upon his arrest, he's simultaneously vilified and martyred. Old ladies deplore "Dirty Abner," and the hipsters (such as they are within this frame of reference) praise the new Hefneresque guru. The magazine becomes more popular than ever, and relocates from its run-down storefront office to posh penthouse headquarters, where a party is thrown in Abner's honor after his release from prison. Ladies sing tribute to him:

> *"Mister Peacock, you're so groovy*
> *What would we ever do without you?*
> *Cary, Rock and Rex* [Harrison?]
> *Have all become Brand X"*

It's nice to look back at the more innocent days of the late '60s, when our biggest concern was magazines that showed women in polka-dotted underwear. Not everyone was part of the counterculture. Some ignored it willfully, like in the previous example; then there were those who only slummed in it. Weekend hippies who tuned in, turned on, dropped out, and went back to work in the morning.

"I love you, Alice B. Toklas
And so does Gertrude Stein
I love you, Alice B. Toklas
And so does Harold Fine"

So begins *I Love You, Alice B. Toklas!*, with the eponymous Harpers Bizarre song over the credits. It's the first movie script by Paul Mazursky, who wrote and/or directed a few other comedies about the zeitgeist from a post-GI/pre–babyboom perspective. The stand-in this time is Harold Fine (Peter Sellers). He has a great future with his law practice and fiancée Joyce (Joyce Van Patten), but something is missing. At least he's not like his hippie brother Herbie (David Arkin). Herbie's old lady Nancy (Leigh Taylor-Young) stays at Harold's house and makes some brownies, the kind reportedly invented by the author in the title, which are later eaten by square Harold and his square in-laws completely oblivious to the "secret" ingredient. This opens Harold's doors of perception wide enough for him to dump his fiancée, shack up with Nancy and fully immerse himself into the life. I won't spoil the ending, but it won't be surprising to anyone familiar with Ambrose Bierce's "An Occurrence at Owl Creek Bridge."

PUSSYCAT, PUSSYCAT, I LOVE YOU (1970)

It's pretty common to remake old movies—but five years later? My own philosophy is that the worse something is, the more acceptable it is to remake. Thus, we come to this remake of *What's New Pussycat?*

The original film was one of Woody Allen's first screenplays. It starred himself as a young man in Paris on the make, Peter O'Toole as another young man in Paris on the make, and Peter Sellers as their sexually frustrated and henpecked psychiatrist. It was a so-so comedy, perhaps most famous for its Tom Jones theme song, and it was remade as an even so-soer comedy. *Pussycat, Pussycat* uses the same premise and as many bars as it can of the original song without violating copyright; it was directed by Rod Amateau, best known for his tenure on *Dobie Gillis.* Severn Darden plays the Sellers role, and is stalked by a gorilla—or, more accurately, by a man in a gorilla suit. As bad as this movie is, I still believe every movie would be improved by a man in a gorilla suit.

LITTLE MURDERS (1971)
FIRE SALE (1977)

Alan Arkin is well known for his acting, but few are aware of his career as director. He only sat in that chair twice, but those two examples prove his talent.

The Jules Feiffer–penned *Little Murders* takes the out-of-towner's bleakest impression of New York City and amplifies it. When Patsy (Marcia Rodd) goes outside to break up a fight and the hoodlums beat her up in turn, the original victim, Alfred (Elliott Gould), walks away. She yells at him for not helping her, and they begin dating. Alfred is a self-described apathist with no opinion or feeling about any situation whatsoever. The only time he ever expresses emotion is when he talks enthusiastically about his art. (He photographs dog shit.)

Men disguised as gorillas factor in several movies.

The courtship of these two is in the forefront while the supporting characters and background become increasingly insane. Patsy's parents (Vincent Gardenia and Elizabeth Wilson) and brother (Jon Korkes) are all funny but not particularly crazy as far as comedies go. Though there are a few over-the-top performances (Donald Sutherland as the "hip" preacher, Arkin as the neurotic Lt. Practice), the insanity is accentuated more by inaction than action. Alfred's personality ends up not being so unique, as some background characters turn out to be just as apathetic, seeming unfazed when fights break out at a wedding or when Alfred rides the subway covered in fresh blood. Even the leading characters gradually become more immune as crime in the streets increases and stray bullets matter-of-factly fly through apartments. Pre-9/11 Manhattan has never been captured so cynically.

Any mention of *Fire Sale* in review books dismisses it with a turkey rating. It's never been released on DVD. And while none of the characters are likeable, that didn't exactly hinder the future acclaim of works by Larry David or the Farrelly Brothers.

Benny Fikus (Gardenia again) and his wife Ruth (Kay Medford) leave for Florida and hand custody of the family store to son Russell (Rob Reiner). Benny stops on the way to give his shell-shocked veteran brother-in-law Sherman (Sid Caesar) instructions to blow up "Nazi Headquarters" (the store) so he can later collect the insurance. Meanwhile, Russell's brother Ezra (Arkin) is an incompetent high-school basketball coach whose wife, Marion (Anjanette Comer), is desperate to have a baby (at one point she locks herself in the refrigerator until he acquiesces). He argues they can't afford it, and he won't go back to work at the store. (Its "Fikus and Son" sign has a prominent silhouette where a plural *S* once was.) When Ezra sees a ghetto teenager playing basketball, he figures that by adopting the kid, he can make his wife happy and make his team win. The problem is that the kid will only comply for a Cadillac. Russell and girlfriend Virginia, unaware of his father's insurance fraud plans, see his absence as an opportunity to improve the dying store and buy new merchandise. Ezra comes crawling back, and the two brothers agree that they can solve their financial problems by cashing in the fire-insurance policy.

Mentioning the many subplots it creates and how they interweave would take the length of this article. Seemingly irrelevant situations become essential. Screenwriter Robert Klane uses the sibling rivalry and senility themes like he did earlier in *Where's Poppa?*—and the plot of the unfunny *Weekend at Bernie's*, which he wrote later, works beautifully when condensed into a five-minute scene here. *Fire Sale* is no *Sullivan's Travels*, but it's hardly the abomination it has been made out to be. (It's possible most critics never saw the movie and plagiarized the one who did to make their books complete.)

POPEYE (1980)

The image the average American has of Popeye is basically Dagwood Bumstead in a sailor suit. Most people groan when I bring up the Robert Altman feature that is perhaps best known as the film where producer Robert Evans was convicted for transporting cocaine, but it's far more faithful to the original material than the later cartoons of the character living in a tract house.

The idea of Altman directing a cartoony movie seems wrong at first. However, a look at the original Max Fleischer cartoons, with mumbled overlapping dialogue and objective point of view, show he's a better match than one might think. Jules Feiffer's script sticks to the premise of the comic, where Popeye actually was a sailor by the sea; it adapts several plotlines from E.C. Segar's run of the strip, including origins of some characters.

A pre-annoying Robin Williams and Shelley Duvall are perfectly cast in the leads, and everyone else looks like they came right out of the comic. An accurate re-creation of the town of

Sweethaven was even built off the coast of Malta. This all has its pluses and minuses. Williams's prosthetic forearms look a bit *too* realistic. And people flying through the air when punched or steam coming out of an angry man's ears don't always translate well to live action. But for every misfire, there's a well-choreographed moment accurately capturing the kinetic energy of animation.

KING FRAT (1979)
UP THE ACADEMY (1980)
SCREWBALLS (1983)

The late '70s and early '80s represent a generational schism in humor. It shows how blatant the difference is between "saying funny things" and "saying things funny." There were movies like *Airplane!* that worked because they were directed and performed in a straight-face style akin to the disaster movies of the time, and *History of the World: Part 1*, which had to constantly let a viewer know it was being funny. It was a weird time for humor: Older comedians, in an attempt to be more like their younger contemporaries, devolved into scatological versions of what they were already doing with limits. Richard Pryor was off-color because he said what he wanted; John Byner was off-color simply because he could be.

The breakthrough hit *Animal House*

King Frat

spawned a new kind of teen movie. The recent surge in '80s nostalgia has made them popular once again, but retrospectives always mention the same pedestrian examples. I prefer the bottom of the barrel.

There were many imitations of *Animal House*, all of which also emulated the Jack Davis school of poster art, in which every cast member is caricatured and every scene from the movie appears on the poster. Despite the shortcomings of most imitations, I must credit them for being more accurate in portraying the squalor associated with most fraternities.

None of these imitations were lower, in production values or content, than *King Frat*. (If I'm wrong, please let me know immediately!) To my knowledge, none of the people involved ever worked on anything else. The movie begins with our beloved Deltas driving around campus mooning people. They see the dean jogging and pick him for their next target, farting in his direction—and killing him! Later, a Rasta brother blows pot smoke into the church vents at the dean's funeral, causing all the mourners to laugh. This is only the first few minutes.

The turning point in the film occurs when J.J. "Gross-Out" Gumbroski, the Belushi stand-in, is reading a newspaper on the toilet and encounters the headline: "FART CONTEST ANNOUNCED!" What's assumed a throwaway sight gag ends up being the main plot to the movie. Gross-Out is a shoo-in for the contest, and to ensure that he wins, the Native American brother has developed a special potion for him to drink backstage. Instead, a dog drinks it and flies across the room. Gross-Out gets disqualified for "drawing mud." To add insult to injury, the victor is his ex-girlfriend.

This movie may seem overly flatocentric, but there's more to it. A rush's first lay at a whorehouse turns out to be the frigid girl he's dating. A gorilla-suited peeping tom accidentally gets "stuck" inside a co-ed. The stereotypical portrayal of blacks and Indians is nonetheless good-natured and reverent, though perhaps overshadowed by an extremely vile and racist gag about

Chinese food (surprisingly, not involving dogs).

Possibly envious of *National Lampoon*'s crossover success with *Animal House*, *MAD* sponsored a movie two years later. Unlike *Animal House*, which was written by *Lampoon* staffers, *MAD* apparently agreed to put its name on a project already being developed by parent company Warner Brothers. *MAD Magazine Presents Up the Academy* was *Animal House* at military school.

Four kids are sent to Weinberg Academy for disgracing their families. One is Chooch (Ralph Macchio), who wants to be a lawyer instead of joining the mob with his dad. Oliver, son of a pro-life mayor, knocked up his girlfriend (Stacey Nelkin, upon whom the Mariel Hemingway character in *Manhattan* is supposedly based), and they're both sent away to salvage his father's re-election. Everyone sneaks out at night and gets caught by the tyrannical Major Liceman (Ron Leibman, who had his credit removed). He threatens to blackmail Oliver, but they turn the tables on him.

Though an obvious imitation of *Animal House*, it's apparent that screenwriters Tom Patchett and Jay Tarses didn't "get" what they were emulating. There's something off about much of the humor, such as the pederastic and predatory Sgt. Sisson (Tom Poston), or the students openly masturbating during a class taught by sexy artillery instructor Miss Bliss (Barbara Bach). Potentially funny gags are ruined by Robert Downey Sr.'s detached direction, which suggests *Airplane!* directed by Robert Altman. This does, however, make for some unintentionally brilliant comedy torture, such as one piece involving a preppy vocal group whose off-key notes break glass in a scene that goes on for three minutes.

Up the Academy closed its first week. The few readers of the comparatively innocuous *MAD* who saw it flooded publisher Bill Gaines with complaints. He sent handwritten apologies to every one of them and paid $30,000 to divorce *MAD* from the film. While *MAD* is left off ancillary packaging, the creepy prosthetic

Alfred E. Neuman remains in the video's titles.

People my age recall *Porky's* fondly, but are usually disappointed when they see it again as adults. Whereas *Porky's* can claim respectability in the name of nostalgia and coming-of-age, *Screwballs* makes no such pretense. *Screwballs*, in other words, is what you think *Porky's* was like.

Four male students at T&A High School are all in detention, along with a cafeteria worker named Mr. Jerkovski (guess why he's there), for actions reported by the chaste Purity Busch. The group forms a bond and decides to get even with her by publicly exposing her breasts somehow, and get sidetracked with all sorts of sexual liaisons and practical jokes in the process.

Leaps in logic abound. One of the students is punished for impersonating the school nurse. He sees fliers for mandatory school breast exams—which feature drawings of bare breasts for the letter *o*—and kidnaps the nurse, taking her place in drag. None of the students seem to suspect anything, let alone recognize him. Far more work is put into planning ways to briefly see girls naked than it would take any guy to get laid in earnest. Girls repulsed by the very presence of Howie, the nerd, have no problem playing strip bowling with him later. Students in detention get away with more than any real person would unsupervised. I can't say my appreciation of this movie is ironic or sincere; it's on some third plane of humor.

A sequel called *Loose Screws* made *Screwballs* look like Molière.

Lowbrow Reader #6 (2008) & #7 (2009)

THE UNFINISHED STOOGES

by Dan Sulman

E VERYONE NOW ASSOCIATES a pie in the face with comedy, but nobody thinks that a pie in the face is funny. How could this be?

To date, conventional wisdom has reconciled pie fact with pie theory by saying that a pie in the face *used* to be funny.

But new evidence, based upon recently discovered manuscripts from the 1930s and '40s—the so-called Golden Age of comedy—suggests that the Three Stooges (perhaps our most notorious pie-hurlers) were not physical comedians, but rather social commentators.

Though these working scripts are difficult to make out because they are covered in pie, what we do have lends itself

Illustration by Doreen Kirchner

to a more humane—and certainly a more verbal—Larry, Moe and Curly. In episode #108, for example, entitled "Moe Hits Curly in the Upper-Left Part of His Head," the climactic custard battle originally was written as a war of words between Moe and Larry over the impending fascist threat.

In one scene, Moe accosts Larry in a stateroom. Larry is dressed as a waiter, though only from the waist up: He has no pants. Moe, on the other hand, is wearing a waiter's trousers, however he is missing a shirt. Conflict ensues. Larry refuses to relinquish his shirt; further, he insists that, as they were invited to the party in the first place, there is no reason to disguise themselves as waiters and sneak in. The episode—a classic—culminates in a naked pie fight. In an alternative version, printed here for the first time, we see a change of tone:

MOE: Nyuk, nyuk, nyuk.

LARRY: [*Threatens with pie.*]

MOE: Nyet. I meant, "Nyet!" Nyet already!

LARRY: So you are a communist after all?

MOE: Yes, anything is better than being a fascist. They are so classless. Just the way the word rolls off one's tongue: Fash-ist. Fashhh-ist. So tacky.

LARRY: And yet, the Germans have no sense for the ethereal.

MOE: Interesting... [*Strokes his chin.*]

It is at this point that Larry slams the pie into Moe's face; the pie fight resumes.

The pie was not a gimmick to be used in performance, but rather, a writing device—shorthand for, "insert something funny here." Pie equals comedy; hence, insert pie. It stuck. They were supposed to go back and rewrite the scenes, but with notoriously rushed production cycles, they inevitably didn't get around to it. {INSERT PIE FIGHT HERE}

Lowbrow Reader #1, 2001

THE MAKING AND UNCOILING OF *PROJECT ACHHH*

by Jay Ruttenberg

A FTER GRADUATING FROM college, I moved into a ratty brown house in Boston along with three friends. They were all nice people, but none were very conscientious when it came to taking out the trash or washing the dishes, and, truth be told, neither was I.

A couple of weeks after moving in, I opened the newspaper classified ads and phoned for the first job that caught my eye. Late-night cookie delivery man. It was similar to being a pizza guy. Every night, people would call our service and order a box of cookies; we would bake the cookies and I would deliver them to the customers' doorsteps, piping hot. I suspect that the damage inflicted to my father's car far surpassed the $30-per-night I was pulling down in tips. Worse, when it came to certain regulars—the 400-pound beast who ordered 24 peanut-butter cookies delivered to his Fenway lair night after night; the panicky heavyweights at MIT, drowning in numbers and butter—I began feeling the guilt that must be familiar to drug dealers. I stayed at the job for about a year and a half.

During this period, my real desire was to write comedy. I was part of a team with my friend Nathan, and every few days we would meet with the intent of writing. Our specific goals were vague. We talked at length about writing for television, though, for much of the time we were working together, neither one of us actually owned a TV. We spoke of writing for the stage, despite the fact that I had never in my life been to the theater. Our other goals included contributing to *MAD* (or, if they wouldn't have us, the ill-famed *Cracked*); writing for *National Lampoon* (which we both failed to notice was no longer publishing); and inducing various acquaintances to perform at comedy clubs, with the foggy notion that we would feed them material.

All of these ambitions were equally far-fetched, if only for the fact that our collected output could have been squeezed into a fortune cookie. Nathan and I didn't write so much as we argued. As the months wore on, our debates became more and more heated, our work less and less productive. I had never considered myself a particularly mean-spirited person, but during the course of our working relationship, I had assumed a bullying role—Nathan took to comparing me to Moe, of the Three Stooges. I would vehemently deny this accusation, then slap Nathan repeatedly across the face and poke my fingers in his eyes. I began to witness an ugly side of myself.

Things took a turn for the worse once Nathan began dating Dana—a randy woman with crooked lipstick whom he met while temping on the outskirts of town. They made an unlikely pair. Dana, more than a decade Nathan's elder, was a recovering alcoholic; Nathan's brushes with drink rarely extended beyond religious dinners. Dana spoke loosely of a troubled past, tainted by a mean '80s rock scene; Nathan had ears only for Billy Joel, who stared at him nightly, through large black sunglasses, from a poster facing his bed. Dana also had a strong aversion to my personality; by the time Nathan met her, so did he.

After a year of watching our friendship deteriorate and our writing efforts come to naught, we decided to record a short comedy album, Project Achhh. It was a last-ditch effort to do something other than exploring creative ways to insult one another's mothers; the moniker was purportedly born of pure absurdity, but I think we both understood it to represent

Nathan / Illustration by Carl Cassel

the frustration we shared with one another. We had a pile of sketches that we thought would work on the record—the lead-off, we decided, would be a short skit about a suburban renaissance teen who informs his pushy parents that he is considering suicide.

Nathan and I decided to record the skit at the office of his psychiatrist, Dr. Goldstein. Nathan was cast as the troubled teen, Dana as his mother and Dr. Goldstein as his father. I will never fully understand what was going through Dr. Goldstein's mind when he agreed to the project. Perhaps he felt some professional obligation to help tug Nathan away from the rut where his life seemed to be headed; perhaps it was a personal diversion, an homage to the Jack Benny routines he claimed to have devoured in his youth. I also suspected that the doctor simply planned on billing the sessions to Nathan's unwitting father. Regardless, Goldstein agreed to host the three of us on a chilly weekday night, in the suburban space where he both lived and saw patients.

I met Nathan and Dana at the North End duplex which they had been sharing since the month prior, when Nathan got into an argument with his roommate, who was black, about the fate of O.J. Simpson—acquitted in court years earlier yet still guilty in my friend's eyes—and was subsequently removed, with a somewhat shocking level of aggression, from the apartment. Dana's place was strange. She lived upstairs, sleeping on the couch by a television set that, to my knowledge, did not have an "off" switch; her sofa was surrounded by magazines about the architectural triumphs of the wealthy. A thin spiral staircase led to a basement room with a requisitely low ceiling. This is where Nathan stayed, rarely sleeping, pacing back and forth in his mad struggle to concoct jokes, sucking the salt from cigar-shaped pretzel sticks. We convened here and exchanged our usual insults. For some reason, I was always yelling at Nathan regarding the sluggish manner in which he walked up stairs, a result of asthma and back problems about which, inexplicably

Dana / Illustration by Carl Cassel

and unforgivably, I had no sympathy. "You lazy putz," I barked. "By the time you get up here, the shrink will be seeing his morning patients."

"You're a real jerk," Nathan replied. "And I bet you forgot the cookies."

Nathan was right on both counts. I had promised to bring a box of cookies from work, but had arrived empty-handed. "My roommates ate them," I countered, my stomach full and head swimming with enough sugar to give my lie the prompt air of truth. "Let's get him something at Dunkin' Donuts."

I removed a stopwatch from my pocket and began timing Nathan's ascent to the ground floor; 17 minutes and 34 seconds later, he had reached the living room and was ready to leave. Dana, Nathan and I walked up the street, past a group of old Italian men playing bocce ball. Nathan and I began to argue about the pronunciation of *bocce*. Then, we got into a profanity-riddled debate about which of the neighborhood's many Dunkin' Donuts would have the freshest Munchkins at that late hour. Dana threw her hands in the air. "Just go to the one on the corner!" she pleaded. "Look, I'll meet you at the car. I'm gonna go buy a soda." Dana made a beeline for the liquor store.

By the time we reached Dr. Goldstein's office, Nathan and I had argued about what to play on the radio, whether we should crack the car window, whether or not Nathan drove worse than Mr. Magoo, the best flavored Munchkin and whether it should be put aside for Dr. Goldstein, whether Dr. Goldstein (whom I had yet to meet) was a homosexual, whether Nathan was a homosexual, whether or not it was prudent for Dana to drink from a brown paper bag when the car was in motion and she was in Alcoholics Anonymous, which person in our circle of acquaintances had the most unpleasant disposition, whether Nathan's boss at Pizzeria Uno was wise to fire him as a server, which one of our mothers would win a chocolate-chip cookie bake-off, and who knows what else. Dana, for her part, was soused. "Why don't you two just shut up and drive," she said, pronouncing "shut up" as *shad ep* and "drive" as *driiiive*. "We gotta go make that funny record with the doctor."

Dr. Goldstein's headquarters, cluttered and inviting, resembled a sitcom rec room more than the sterile psychiatric offices of popular imagery. He was a slim man with the slender, nervous fingers of a teenage boy and the silver hair of a gentleman. The shrink and his patient greeted one another with winking familiarity, like war veterans who had once shared a foxhole. Dana, who had taken to accompanying Nathan to his afternoon sessions, smiled brightly at Goldstein and pressed the box of Munchkins tightly against his chest. "Here're your doughnuts, Doc," she said. "We got 'em for you at Dunkin'."

The doctor eyed me with suspicion. If a thought balloon were to float from his head, I think it would have read, "This guy doesn't seem all that bad." We exchanged pleasantries. Dana burped.

The argument that ultimately would define and demolish our recording experience erupted soon after we showed Goldstein the script, "Suicidal Aspirations." The sketch featured three characters: a mother and father, respectively played by Dana and the shrink, and their teenage son, to be portrayed by Nathan. It was a short bit: The couple sit in bed, both reading John Updike books. Their son enters the room and informs them that he has a problem. "Is it the tennis team?" the father asks. "It's your backhand, isn't it?" The son calmly tells his parents that his issue is more severe, and the mother assumes the worst. "A B+ isn't that bad!" she says. "I know it's not Ivy League material, but we'll work with the math tutor." Actually, the son calmly explains, he has been thinking of committing suicide. His parents are naturally supportive. "The Rosenberg child hung himself and left an absolutely *charming* note behind," the mother explains. "I was talking to his mother yesterday— why, she said it was better than his college essays! 'If he had sent *that note to Yale*,' Mrs. Rosenberg said, 'he would have been accepted in a heartbeat!' So if you want to go over your suicide note with the English tutor first, just let us know. Or I can help you with it!" Eventually, the parents persuade their son to postpone his suicide until he has completed his final exams and that year's tennis season.

Dr. Goldstein read the script, to which he had so foolishly committed himself. He looked at us dourly. The brazen inappropriateness of his participation had dawned on him—you could see the distressing realization in his face, the way his panicky eyes darted around the room as if searching for an escape

Dr. Goldstein / Illustration by Carl Cassel

hatch. Normally, he commanded this office like some authoritarian king; now he was outnumbered, surrounded by fools and drunks. He returned to the short script and began rapidly clicking his tongue against the roof of his mouth, creating an irritating sound meant to indicate thought. At last, he seized on his potential exemption: The parents in the sketch had been named after Nathan's parents in real life. Apparently, this set off some psychiatric red flag.

Of course, the characters' names had no significance whatsoever—they were put in as placeholders, much as the pseudonyms "Nathan," "Dr. Goldstein" and "Dana" function here. Yet so accustomed were Nathan and I to battling over every last detail of life that we mindlessly leapt at this opportunity to skirmish with the doctor. "This is how it's written," Nathan said, suddenly exuding the frustrated air of a grizzled Hollywood vet. "Why can't you just read your lines?"

"It goes against the ethics of my profession to participate in this kind of Oedipal reference," the psychiatrist responded, conveniently ignoring the fact that Oedipal references served as the very foundation of his trade.

"You're being a cunt!" Nathan exclaimed.

"I'm being a cunt?" Dr. Goldstein responded. He spoke with extraordinary cool, as if not even bullets could unnerve him. Dana and I, suddenly united in our astonishment, both froze. It was as if our notion of psychiatry had just been dismissed, then rewritten by Redd Foxx. "I don't think it's right," Goldstein went on. "I don't think it's proper to—*in public*—defame your mother that way. You can say whatever you want in private, do whatever you want in private—"

"But this is funny!" Dana yelled, her voice raised to a volume typically reserved for criticizing a professional hockey player. "His mother would think this was funny!"

"How do you know?" the doctor asked.

"Because I know his mother!" Dana said. "I know her pretty well. She would think this is funny."

"Dr. Goldstein's in love with my mother," Nathan snapped, "so I think he has more of a feeling on this one."

The doctor hemmed and hawed, straining to convince himself that he maintained some measure of control over the situation. Ultimately, he acquiesced—though the few times that the script called for his character to refer to his wife, he childishly fudged the name. It didn't matter. The comedy record was a flop, just like everything else Nathan and I did. We would play it for friends and receive looks of befuddlement and sympathy. I had hoped that the anarchic premise of Project Achhh would help us tap the intimacy and unpredictability that attracted me to home-recorded rock albums. But the berserk circumstances of its creation were not reflected in the work itself, which was muddled, shticky and unfunny—like something little kids would record.

A few months after our encounter with the psychiatrist, Nathan and Dana broke up. Nathan stopped seeing Dr. Goldstein, labeling the doctor a "quack," and moved to Los Angeles, where he met Mel Brooks while both men were shopping for sneakers. Then, he returned to Boston. He performs standup comedy intermittently and, from what I hear, he's quite funny. I am not surprised. I always felt the rancor inherent to our working relationship stifled his ingenuity.

I left Boston long ago, spending a lonely year out West before settling in New York. I no longer deliver cookies; sometimes, I miss the hint of freedom that came with the job, but I suppose we all must move on. Nathan and I talk to each other from time to time, but we rarely broach our shared failure, Project Achhh. We don't argue anymore, either. Nowadays, I save that for family, neighbors, co-workers, tennis partners and strangers I encounter on the street. Sometimes I wonder how life would have turned out had Nathan and I been more successful in our comedic endeavors. I envision us speeding down L.A. freeways in foreign-built convertibles, sipping lavish cocktails with Alfred E. Neuman, holding our own in pie fights against descendents of the Three Stooges. But mostly, I just picture us in a nasty state of constant bicker, hampered by years of misguided antipathy and sloth that not even a doctor could cure.

Lowbrow Reader #6, 2008

SUPPOSING MOSES:
A NOVEL OF ART

by Jay Jennings

T O THE WORLD, she was Grandma, but I—her lover, her
model, her muse—called her by a more affectionate term
of endearment: Granny.

We dropped the formality as quickly as we dropped our
clothes shortly after I arrived to model for her in her studio on
the Left Bank. Postwar Paris was reeling from the '40s, I was
barely out of my teens, and she was well into her 80s. As so
many young men had in those days, I had come to Paris to write
a novel (we even chartered a flight). At 21, I was innocent of the
ways of the world but assured of my eventual greatness. Until
some editor discovered my florid, ineluctable talent, however, I
hired out as a model. In my favor, I had the bronzed skin, chis-
eled physique and outsize head of a Rodin statue. Unfortunately,
Giacometti was all the rage, and I had trouble getting work.

Then, one morning in a café, I came upon an ad in *Le Monde*,
under the section "Help Wanted for Aspiring Novelists in Paris."
It read: "Artist's model needed. Extremely naïve. 14 Rue des
Fleurs." I fit the description to a T, so I downed my espresso,
finished off my madeleine, bid adieu to Simone and Jean-Paul,
and sought out the address.

As I arrived at the dingy building, another young novelist,
whom I recognized from the charter, was scurrying down the
stairs, naked, his clothes bundled in his arms. A glass jar of

paint, thrown from a landing above, smashed behind him, leaving a Van Gogh sunburst of yellow on the wall, where it joined other different colored splotches.

"Get out, you art brut!" a voice shouted from the landing above. "And don't come back!"

With some trepidation, I ascended the stairs. And there she was, framed in the doorway of her studio loft: the great Grandma Moses. She despised being called "the great Grandma Moses" because she insisted she was not old enough to be a great-grandma. From the time that I first met her, she was always concerned that her looks were fading, that age was causing her powers to erode, but I tried to reassure her by telling her that although she was well into her 80s, she looked as if she were only barely into her 80s. Even these comforting words did little to give her solace, and there followed another of her inevitable drinking binges and explosions of temper.

As I continued up the stairs, she raised a can of turpentine to her lips and took a huge swig. "Ah, fresh meat," she said, and motioned for me to enter.

"Get undressed," she immediately demanded. And when I did, she let out a loud gasp. It was her emphysema, the result of a lifetime of smoking unfiltered Gitanes. But as I was to find out, there was still life in her yet, before she would become a still life.

She worked incessantly, fanatically, doing hours of studies before she would finally settle in front of a canvas. She covered pages of sketchbooks with stick figures, trying to get the correct placement of the arms and legs. "Not naïve enough!" she shouted at the top of her lungs and would toss into the fire drawings that would now fetch a fortune at auction. Out of these studies came her greatest (and now lost) work, *Hangman*, a simple but moving reflection on death—which some experts believe to be a self-portrait—in the form of a one-legged figure dangling from a gallows, over the heartbreakingly incomplete signature below: G R A N D _ A _ O S E S.

Of course, we became lovers. After a day of posing and painting, in the dim light of the loft, we made wild love on her pallet. Sometimes, when we rolled off the pallet, we made love on her palette. And inevitably, in our passionate thrashings, on her upper palate, which fell out during one of our marathon sessions.

But it was not all roses with Moses. She was given to despair. One day, after working on an enormous canvas, we ordered out Chinese. She stopped between bites of an egg roll and said suddenly, with a fierce intensity, waving her arm at her painting, "This will be my Last Supper!"

Illustration by Mike Reddy

Again, I tried to reassure her. "Don't talk that way, Granny. You've got a good two years left, at least."

How wrong I was! In fact, she would live another 15 years, to the age of 101. And in those last years of her life, her art changed dramatically. Casting me off as she had hundreds of other young lovers, she returned to New England, destroying the works that I posed for and all others from that rich, formative time (Early Youth, 1860–1946) before creating the bucolic, and dare I say sentimental, landscapes for which she is best known today (The Blue Hair Period, 1947–1961). How might contemporary art be different had those modernist masterpieces

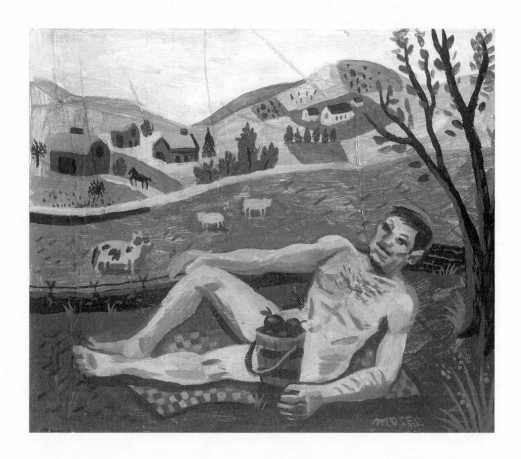

survived? How might the world be different if we'd had those works to communicate our existential angst? It's impossible to say, but the loss is surely great. As no less a genius than Beckett exclaimed to me once during a visit to her studio, "Grandma, c'est moi."

And by the same author, here's an excerpt from the forthcoming Norman Conquest: A Novel of Norman Rockwell.

There's a good reason Norman was named Rockwell, because after a day of tagging subway cars, he frequented the punk clubs of the East Village. I was playing in a band called the Stockbridge Stranglers....

Lowbrow Reader #4, 2004

THE CASE AGAINST CHASE
by Ben Goldberg

NOTHING IS MORE pathetic than feeling shame for a movie actor. I still remember spotting the poster for *Funny Farm* and being embarrassed for its principle star, Chevy Chase. There he was, an oversized guy driving a miniaturized tractor, with a face like he was about to crash into a bale of hay, while a backseat dog stuck its head out behind him. It's that all-too-common moment when somebody you respected in pop culture has crossed the degradation boundary for a check. My immediate reaction was to clench my teeth, groan and hope this marked a momentary dip into the kids movie pool—perfectly respectable when done once a decade or so. No luck. Chevy, I felt, had fallen from the high stature I always felt for him.

This happened before I realized two important facts: One, Chevy Chase is a tremendous asshole. And two, he was almost *never* funny. While the first is obvious if you've ever seen or read an interview with him (or, perhaps more notably, with anybody who has worked with him), the second may be more surprising. What about *Fletch*? What about *SNL*? *Vacation*? Well, what people recall as Chase-ian humor is most often not him, or only a good line amid nonsense, and his career has two distinct halves, only notable as a whole because Eddie Murphy must have used it to follow a similar path. What you might have thought was there in 1981 wasn't really there—and if it was there, it was the tiniest nugget, exploited by its perpetrator beyond all respectability. The awful reality is that Fletch is dead, the Griswolds have gone home and Gerald Ford is having the last laugh.

CHEVY CHASE IS A JERK
(AND EVERYBODY KNOWS IT)

Chevy-bashing is nothing new. Some years ago, a Friars Club roast provided its own special insult by offering oddly little-known comedians to hurl insults at Chase. Why didn't the more high-profile comics the guest of honor has worked with through his career show up? Could it be they've never heard of the Friars Club? Or did the notion of a good-natured lambasting of Chase not particularly appeal to them? We also have *Live from New York*, an oral history of *Saturday Night Live* that shows Chase's bullying behavior toward pretty much everyone around him. This isn't just demanding some alone time in the dressing room: Chase is described by gay comedian Terry Sweeney as suggesting a sketch where Sweeney plays a dying AIDS patient who gradually loses weight; female writers note how he's crude and brash, requesting "hand jobs" as a means of intimidating

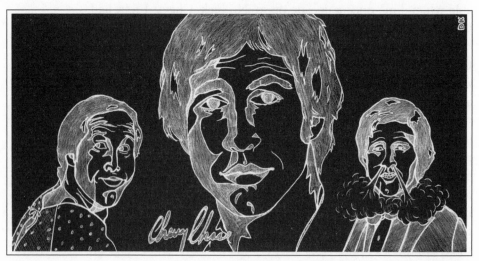

Illustration by Doreen Kirchner

them. He's that special brand of human who, handed the brass ring of celebrity, appears to have shoved it up his own ass, then forced others around him to smell it.

CHEVY CHASE IS NOT CARY GRANT

Chase was the first of the *SNL* group to get into movies, and the ones he did were pretty good. *Caddyshack, Foul Play, Seems Like Old Times* and *Under the Rainbow* are all funny. But he's never in the comic scenes, at least as the focal point of humor. Instead, he managed to tailor his roles as attractive protagonists, emerging from the films as the effortlessly clever guy amid the boobs. And he wasn't there to be part of the laughs as much as to forward typical '80s movies plots. Compare this to Cary Grant, who managed not only to be a suave sex symbol, but also was able to offer pitch-perfect (and self-effacing) comic timing in films like *Bringing Up Baby, His Girl Friday* and *The Philadelphia Story.* Chase tried playing it the same way, as the comic who always came off not just lovable but looking damn good. And as long as he was cast with talented people, nobody noticed that he was not particularly noteworthy. Chase was all business acumen when deciding to do these films, but hardly brought anything to them of his own. He kept having *serious love scenes* in his movies—talk about a humor kill! Conversely, you probably remember Dudley Moore's sex-starved bachelor in *Foul Play*, the army of dogs ruining the dinner party in *Old Times*, all the funny little people in *Rainbow*—and, of course, Bill Murray's legendary groundskeeper in *Caddyshack*.

CHEVY CHASE TAKES A ROLE HE PROBABLY CONSIDERS OKAY TO DO JUST ONCE

As early as 1981, the future Chase legacy could be glimpsed in *Modern Problems*, a movie that I found absolutely brilliant when I was eight. Chevy gets telekinetic powers and can make people

268 | THE LOWBROW READER READER

do funny things, like get excessive nosebleeds in restaurants. *Modern Problems* is possibly the most noteworthy film of his career, because it is here that we get the first glimpse of that wonderful face with which we will become so familiar: The one where Chase purses his lips, widens his eyes and pushes back his cheeks. In a sense, it was the '80s comic complement to Andrew McCarthy's you-must-believe-how-serious-I-am-right-now face and ultimately became abused even more than Murphy's good-natured guffaw.

Fletch, from 1985, was the pinnacle of his suave persona, and it came, not surprisingly, a year after *Beverly Hills Cop* popularized the approach (in the first half of his career, Chase made great business decisions). Chase is all one-liners, offering clever repartee with his female costar and gently mocking everyone else around him. He's smooth as baby poo, and it takes the alternately wacky and excessively normal characters around him to excel at getting material off them—the standard setup for nearly every television sitcom ever made.

This road actually left him with possibilities given the success of *Vacation*, where his *Modern Problems* persona really took root. Yet again, Chevy benefits from a funny script and also surrounds himself with very funny people, like John Candy and, in the sequel, Eric Idle. Unlike his early movies, however, he was no longer the suave guy but the punch line—a George Clooney turned Homer Simpson. A significant change was afoot, for he was quickly abandoning any dignity, and the good scripts were disappearing.

CHEVY CHASE HOSTS THE LAMEST LATE-NIGHT SHOW EVER MADE

How lousy was it? On the first night, Goldie Hawn picked up a microphone and sang Chevy a torch song. The rookie host had no idea how to react. For an excruciating three minutes, he glazed his eyes, pulled back at the ends of his mouth and lifted his forehead; then, he would attempt to earnestly enjoy it, only to return to the face. If he were still in *Modern Problems*, everyone in the audience would have suffered hemorrhaging nosebleeds, but luckily, in real life he's not that talented.

CHEVY CHASE DESPERATELY DOES ANYTHING TO KEEP HIS FILM CAREER GOING

They become a blur: *Funny Farm, Cops and Robbersons, Man of the House, Memoirs of an Invisible Man*…all reaching dirt bottom with *Vegas Vacation*.

By this point, the doddering, gurgling, eyes-glazing Chase has lost all control of career direction and accepts any role barfed up to him. "Well, at least he only appeared in one movie with an animal sidekick," one might note. Sorry to say, that would be neglecting 1980's *Oh! Heavenly Dog*, in which Chase costarred with Benji.

THANK GOD CHEVY CHASE LEFT *SNL* TO MAKE ROOM FOR BILL MURRAY

Bill Murray played the buffoon early on in *Caddyshack* and *Meatballs*, got a few wiseass roles in *Ghostbusters* and *Stripes*, and sealed the deal by deftly playing both types at once in *Groundhog Day*. Then, he did the impossible—at least impossible to think of at the time of *The Razor's Edge*—by showing himself to be, ultimately, the brilliant actor of *Rushmore* and *Lost in Translation*. Not only that, but the only person who seems to think *he's* an asshole is Lucy Liu, which makes him all the more likeable. Hell, I even like Brian Doyle-Murray because of Bill!

Murray got his big chance because Chase left *SNL* after one year—the two men famously did not get along, and once even sparred backstage. Recently, during a panel surveying his film career at the Brooklyn Academy of Music, Murray was encouraged by an audience member to disparage Chase. The crowd laughed, and Murray said, "This is so easy." But after admitting the strangeness of his former rival's career decisions, Murray praised Chase for being funny in real life. ("Spend a day with me, and you'll be glad just to survive," he said, by comparison, of himself.)

One can understand Murray's sliver of fondness for Chevy, whose year on *SNL* still contains Chase's two most memorable contributions to pop culture: his mock anchor at the news desk and his impression of Gerald Ford. As anchor, Chase cast a believable glow—the straight man just a little bit off. He kept a stone face, reigning in the humor from becoming too wacky, and caused shrieks of guffaws for his practice of taking personal calls in the midst of a telecast. Chase's Gerald Ford was a one-joke act, falling down, but it was clever, particularly since Chase didn't make any attempt to look or sound like Ford. The joke lay in the pure anticipation of when he'd topple over and what would cause it. Right at the start, the great arc of his career was played out in miniature. Chase enters the scene respectable and dignified, the consummate straight man contextually funny because he's on a comedy show, and everyone just waits for the clownish fall. His career inevitably led to that punch line; when he finally embraced it, he quickly became it.

Eventually, the nostalgia will fade, and the film roles that made Chevy Chase a viable commodity will be forgotten. He serves as the negative What If scenario for Garrett Morris and Lorraine Newman, who can be thankful they walked away from *Saturday Night Live* with their dignity, if little work. Chevy himself will be remembered best for his associations, which will rub off when people aren't really giving thought to it. But those who do will remember what little he contributed to American humor and do their best to eliminate this living Jar Jar Binks from their minds.

Lowbrow Reader #5, 2006

THE CASE FOR CHASE
by Joe O'Brien

I KNOW CHEVY'S a prick. I've seen the *Saturday Night Live* book, the Friars Club roast. I'm not blind to the smug, puffy-eyed ego. I know he's had the wacky pratfall routine on speed-dial for years. I know that many of his performances could have been handled with equal aplomb by a cigar-store Indian.

Chevy's been zinged good. Michael O'Donoghue called him "a giant garden slug" and predicted, when they first met in the '70s, that "someday [Chevy] will be a mediocre movie star." Stephen Colbert has called him "a pear-shaped husk, a comedy lamprey that sucks the joy out of everything it touches." Bill Murray, after coming to blows with Chevy backstage at *SNL*, delivered what is perhaps one of entertainment's greatest insults when he called his rival a "medium talent." Even Burt Reynolds took a swipe at Chase. When Reynolds was a guest on the short-lived *Chevy Chase Show*, he complained about how Loni Anderson was publicly discussing their breakup. When Chevy accused him of doing the same thing, Reynolds zapped him with "Yeah, but nobody's watching." Rimshot!

Anyone with a handy copy of Chase's recent filmography can see why poor bastards like me, who still like the comic, have had to undergo the transformation from fan to apologist. Recently, I reviewed some of my favorite Chevy movies and also took into consideration some of his later, universally panned work. While *Cops and Robbersons'* Norman Robberson may not stack up against *Caddyshack*'s Ty Webb or *Vacation*'s Clark W. Griswold, and while I couldn't even muster the effort to track down the recent *The Karate Dog*, in most cases I can safely and honestly blame the movies, not Chevy. The odd thing with Chase, however, is that he doesn't bother to outshine the material: He clearly doesn't give a rat's ass. He's like the sourpuss waiter at Shoney's who walks around bad-mouthing the dinner specials. Bad for morale, sure—but at least he's honest.

Chevy's never done the simpering, sappy act. He's never made me sick to my stomach the way Billy Crystal or Mike Myers have. He's never offended every aspect of my sensibility, like Robin Williams or Paul Reiser have. Even in the sentimental family fare he favors, Chevy manages to exude an air of sour disinterest, which can be oddly refreshing.

At his best, Chevy is a gifted physical comedian who's also capable of beautifully delivering an absurd line. In *Caddyshack*, when he informs a judge's niece, "your uncle molests collies," there isn't another actor who could've said it better. *Fletch* is another prime example of Chevy's talent—his timing and throwaway delivery is flawless, and nearly every joke lands

Illustration by Doreen Kirchner

on its feet. It's Chevy riding the fence between broad, mugging slapstick and more subtle verbal comedy. The aliases are great—Mr. Poon, John Cocktoasten—and when he wakes up on a hospital couch, identifies himself as Dr. Rosenrosen and demands the head of Alfredo Garcia, well, that's pretty damn funny.

Caddyshack, *Fletch* and the perennially underrated *Christmas Vacation* are evergreens that never tire. But those movies are all in the past; now, we must look to the future.

There have been wiser decisions than Chase turning down

SOME LITTLE-KNOWN FACTS ABOUT CHEVY CHASE

- Became addicted to painkillers as a result of the acrobatic pratfalls that brought him fame.

- Every year, serves as Grand Marshal for the July 4th parade in Chevy Chase, Maryland.

- Named his firstborn son Garrett Chase in honor of Garrett Morris, his confidant at *Saturday Night Live*.

- Struggled for years to get published in *MAD* magazine, ultimately succeeding with a short piece spoofing *Mission Impossible*. ("He never came into our office and didn't do a pratfall," Nick Meglin, the magazine's long-time editor, told *Lowbrow*. "He got us every time.")

- Is known in Finland as "Pepsi Man" due to his role, since 1979, as the Finnish face of Pepsi Cola.

- First found notoriety for his work in "You're Late Again, Rock Hard," a National Lampoon Radio Hour bit in which Chase played the harried boss of a pizza delivery boy/porn star.

the Kevin Spacey role in *American Beauty* (arguing he only wanted to do "family movies"). Yes, the comedian's instinct might have led him to do the old bug-eye routine when he saw Mena Suvari in a bathtub full of rose petals, or stumble over the couch after smoking marijuana. For the most part, however, Chevy would have been great in the picture.

If I were Chase's agent, I would say: "Chevy, you've gotta start playing to your strengths. Screw the family films. You're an asshole, so you should play an asshole. You're too old for slapstick—and nobody accepts you as the nice family man anymore. I don't know what's stopping you. You've got plenty of money. Your reputation is completely shot. What the hell do you have to lose?"

I'd like to see Chevy embrace his inner bastard—cast as a bitter drunk, an aloof father or a passive-aggressive husband who terrorizes his wife with petty criticisms. Have him dig into that dark side that he only hinted at with the ill will and disdain that was at the root of his role in *Funny Farm* (itself an overlooked gem).

I know that I'm not objective. I have a soft spot for wasted talents and human shipwrecks. But I'm convinced that Chevy's day will come again. All he needs is one solid role in a movie that they won't let him ruin with a sequel.

The people who hate Chevy have much more ammunition than us loyalists—he's too easy a target, a critic's piñata hanging helplessly alongside Carrot Top and Rod Stewart. But I'm convinced that the joke will ultimately be on Chase's detractors—that the miserable sonofabitch will once again be able to take some pride in the fact that he's Chevy Chase and we're not.

Lowbrow Reader #5, 2006

A MEMO TO ALL PARTNERS AND ASSOCIATES

by Jay Ruttenberg

As THOSE OF you who consult the daily newspaper's business section may already know, Berger, Mednick and Salerno has recently been acquired by Anderson, Herald and Willis. The reasons for the merger are varied, though mainly have to do with departing Office Manager Robert Levy, who, we have recently learned, is a mental lunatic. One would think that the madness of one Office Manager would not infiltrate so venerable an institution, but it seems that during his decades with the firm Mr. Levy had more sway than many partners realized.

Obviously, changes around the office are inevitable. Use this memo as a provisional guide for the newly formed Anderson, Berger, Herald, Mednick, Salerno and Willis.

• Please discard all copies of the Employee Handbook's chapter on Sexual Harassment, which, it turns out, merely compiles scripts from old Miller Genuine Draft commercials. A new Sexual Harassment policy will be issued in coming weeks; in the meantime, please refrain from talking to or about any member of the opposite sex. Also, please refrain from partaking in sexual intercourse on the floor of the office disco.

• Until further notice, there will be no more Bring Your Child to Work Day. There also will be no more Bring Your Recently

Laid-Off Paralegal to Work Day, Let the Janitorial Staff Woo the Clients Day, Pretend We're a Winning Football Squad and the Boss Is Coach Day, or Do No Work at Work Day. Please change your schedules accordingly.

• Say goodbye to morning receptionists Todd Bridges and Gary Coleman; say hello to morning receptionists Lena Austin and Sofia Harris! Both come to us from the WCL Temping Agency and have vast professional reception experience.

• No doubt, you will notice empty chairs where the Office Flirt, Office Scapegoat and Office Gossip once toiled. As it turns out, these positions are typically filled by people already employed at a workplace in a more traditional capacity. If any attorney is interested in assuming one of these roles in addition to his or her usual tasks, please see Human Resources about the possibility of salary adjustments and the slackening of normal workloads.

• For those attorneys who take lunch at the desk, our beloved baseball park–style weenie vendors will no longer be making the office rounds. Furthermore, the kitchenette is not to be used for pig roastings, live tapings of *Iron Chef* or the baking of pies for our monthly pie-eating/pie-hurling face-offs with the District Attorney's office.

• The DVD law library of *My Cousin Vinny*, *To Kill a Mockingbird*, *Law Students Gone Wild!!!* and *Aerobicizing with Alan Dershowitz* will hereby be replaced with proper legal texts decorated with florid leather spines. NOTE: Our cable hook-up, which we are informed is of the illegal variety, will be shut off within the next three and a half years. We apologize for any inconvenience this may cause.

• You will notice casual Fridays assuming a less casual tone. Consulting with other offices around the city, we have learned that this day is not meant to be interchangeable with Halloween, Mardi Gras, or Day of the Dead. Civil War military garb is hereby banned until further notice, along with all Bozo the Clown wear and vintage pornographic eyeglasses.

• Naturally, there will be several changes in regard to the water cooler. Past experiments filling it with Strawberry Yoo-hoo or crushed chocolate-chip cookies were no doubt good for office morale, but the tank will now be reserved strictly for water. When the tank is empty, please see a member of the firm's maintenance department about replacing it—the tri-daily "office strongman" competitions of the past frequently left the floor flooded and, as with the office chicken coop, encouraged gambling. (Please note that our health insurance plan will no longer

Illustration by Carl Cassel

cover hernias suffered while lifting large jugs of water.)

• On a similar note, some information has come across our desk concerning the television sensation known as the "Water Cooler Moment." As you will learn in next week's mandatory workshop with executives from the UPN network, the intent of this phenomenon is to discuss highlighted moments of programs— not to stage theatrical re-creations of *The Osbournes* or *Blind Date* at the water cooler.

• Please refrain from chasing the office mice while in the presence of opposing counsel.

• Though it remains billable, working long hours in a dream does not substitute for actual time spent at work. Furthermore, all attorneys must report to work following nightmares that take place at the office, even if the dream is "really, really scary."

• We have found that when dealing with clients, it is best to limit conversations to the one- to two-second range when discussing the following topics:

> • The spiritual significance of a new tattoo
> • The forbidden thrill of chasing office mice while in the presence of opposing counsel
> • Diarrhea
> • The relative softness of motorcyclists who ride foreign-manufactured vehicles
> • The motivational speech delivered to the firm last summer by Eminem
> • Our recently departed Office Manager, Robert Levy

• Finally, while we realize that many associates spent valuable hours constructing the lobby's rubberband-ball rendering of Abe Mednick, management has requested that it be replaced with a tinfoil portrait of incoming senior partner Herbert S. Willis. Tinfoil can be collected from the office cafeteria—né, Robert Levy's Opium Den—each day around 2 pm (formerly "The Napping Hour").

Unless otherwise noted, all changes are effective immediately.

Lowbrow Reader #3, 2003

CREDITS

Marie Antoinette	Gwyneth Paltrow
Ralph the Guard	Rob Schneider
Louis XVI	Colin Firth
Maria Theresa	Frances McDormand
Erich Von Klost	Thierry Lhermitte
Villager #1	Zachary Stewart
Villager #2	David Garté
Monique the Poodle	Himself
Tom Vlapid	Billy Frazier
Grip	Jim Gonzalez
Boom Mic Operator	Michael S. Binder
Director's assistant	Allie McCain
Ms. Paltrow's assistant	Daisy Simon
Mr. Schneider's assistant	Becky Heinl
Mr. Schneider's assistant	Jason Chapin
Mr. Schneider's assistant	Jules Young
Mr. Schneider's nude double (back)	Evan Rouser
Mr. Schneider's nude double (front)	Shaquille Jones
Mr. Schneider's stand-in for mingling with local "losers"	Matthew Fider
Mr. Schneider's (harried) acting coach	Elizabeth Grossman

Mr. Schneider chauffeured to and from set on the shoulders of	Naomi Belvaux
Mr. Schneider's entourage provided by	Insta-Diva Entourage, Inc.
Mr. Schneider's security provided by	Steele Security, Inc.
Steele Security Inc.'s security provided by	O'Flannery Security, Inc.
Man responsible for holding Mr. Schneider's monocle and cape during on-set temper tantrums	Charles Hershey
Man who sits at restaurants with Mr. Schneider to tell him what a good orderer he is	Josh Rudinski
Scholar responsible for translating Mr. Schneider's lines to his native Pig Latin	Andrew Zankel, Ph.D.
Zen Master retained to remind Mr. Schneider not to yell at parents over the telephone	Ira Wu Bong Nim
Man who tells Mr. Schneider what to think about while falling asleep for the night	Brad Wolfe
Researcher hired to investigate the ways Ms. Paltrow has been successfully bedded by co-stars	Rebecca Bing
Underage cancer patient paid to request Make-a-Wish excursion with Mr. Schneider	Steven Treude
Scapegoat prepared to accept blame when Mr. Schneider soils pants	Ed Romanonski
Employee responsible for reminding Mr. Schneider not to drink milk with breakfast burritos	Ed Romanonski
Cobbler who provides special footwear for Mr. Schneider (who must be no taller than 4'5" offscreen)	Grant Werner
Irish thug responsible for sucker-punching paparazzi photogs who fail to capture Mr. Schneider's "good" side	James O'Malley
Nutritionist hired by Mr. Schneider's mother to surreptitiously add vegetables to his daily crouton salad	Kate Kindred
Mr. Schneider's toenails styled by	Nicolas Thunder

Man who covers Mr. Schneider's ears when he drops the toilet seat in an echoey bathroom	Scott Gilmore
Computer technician working on improving Mr. Schneider's Google count	Jerry Aubele
Doctor responsible for assuring Mr. Schneider there is nothing wrong with the way his testicles hang from his scrotum	Charles Peckman, MD
Think tank consulted to concoct catch phrase for Mr. Schneider	Werner & Jones
Script doctor hired to insert the expression "Les pajamas? Oui!" at dramatic pinnacles of film	Alan London
Ghostwriter trailing Mr. Schneider to gather inspiration for the forthcoming children's book "Rob Schneider's The Little Snail by Rob Schneider"	Georgia Marino
Psychiatrist retained to study behavioral patterns of Oscar-night losers	Caroline Wright
Church of Scientology elder who tells Mr. Schneider where he stands on various issues	Owen Robinson
Interesting person who feeds Mr. Schneider stories to recount on Conan	Allison Smith
Chemist hired to mix Mr. Schneider's Breath O' Heather Vat 106 Plus	Wendy Crawford
Best Boy	J.R. Miller

With the exception of two or three small cats that were kicked by Mr. Schneider during one of his crystal meth and Frappuccino–fueled frenzies, no animals were harmed in the making of this film.

Lowbrow Reader #4, 2004

ACKNOWLEDGMENTS

Wow. What a tremendous honor. I mean, *woo!* Yeah! [*Ruttenberg smugly scans the audience from his lofted position on the dais, then takes a moment to covetously eye his trophy.*] Thank you! Thank you, fans! And thank you, Academy! This is all so surprising—who would have ever imagined? [*The speaker removes from his tuxedo jacket a heavily annotated paper and makes a show of unfolding his prepared remarks.*] To begin on a personal note, I would like to thank Francesca, without whom I would be worthless plankton, bowed in fetal position in some trashy Podunk, surely disheveled and possibly soiled. Let me also thank my parents, who return my calls in good years and bad, as well as my brother, who does not. These people are all hilarious, and I am fortunate to know them. Furthermore, let me salute my in-laws in Italy and friends in New York and beyond. [*Ruttenberg theatrically pauses as he awaits applause; little is forthcoming.*] The *Lowbrow Reader* is very much a collective experience. I am endlessly appreciative of the work supplied by every individual involved. These mensches include the writers and artists who contributed to this book as well as to the eight issues and the website, plus the musicians and comedians who have performed at the Lowbrow Reader Variety Hour shows. At this point, I would like to single out for the highest of praise Matthew Berube, who stands behind me on this elegant dais but is too modest to speak. [*Berube approaches the foot of the stage. "Actually," he begins, "I would like to take a moment to thank Suenita, Violet, Jack and—" Ruttenberg elbows Berube aside and brusquely reclaims the microphone.*] Matt has been a true partner in the *Lowbrow*

Reader, working in a role that begins as designer but extends far beyond that capacity. I cannot thank him enough. As with Matt, John Mathias and Neil Hagerty worked on *Lowbrow Reader* #1 all the way through the most recent issue and this anthology. Both helped shape the *Lowbrow* more than they realize, and have offered consistently dazzling and surprising contributions. [*Hagerty takes a step up on the podium and opens his mouth to speak; Ruttenberg deftly bats him aside.*] If you have even casually flipped through this book, you have no doubt marveled at the plentiful illustrations of Mike Reddy, whose contributions over the years have proved invaluable. As if that is not enough, he has helped to mold articles and, from deep within the nefarious trenches of *Seventeen* magazine, lent technical assistance. [*"Thank you, to my colleagues at Banos—" Reddy begins, before tumbling from the stage as Ruttenberg wrestles the microphone away from his clutches through the introduction of his knee to the artist's groin.*] Of course, the list of worthy souls runs much longer; it includes every person on this book's contents page and many more. Finally, I cannot believe the *Lowbrow Reader's* good fortune in ending up in the hands of Drag City, a company that years ago changed the way I listened to music and digested culture. I am honored and humbled that this book has joined Drag City's ranks. I thank Dan Koretzky, Dan Osborn, Scott McGaughey, and the rest of the staff at America's greatest cultural production house. [*The speaker ostentatiously struggles to hold back a tear, ultimately succeeding with the aid of a conspicuously displayed silk handkerchief.*] Indeed, it has been a long evening. And so I now leave you with an aphorism widely credited to the great Harpo Marx— [*As Ruttenberg prattles on, his microphone goes dead and, mercifully, the orchestra's exit music ushers him offstage.*]

INDEX

NOTES ON CONTRIBUTORS

DAVID BERMAN, of Nashville, released six albums with his band the Silver Jews. He is the author of a book of poetry, *Actual Air*, and a book of cartoons, *The Portable February*.

Veteran comedian SHELLEY BERMAN has appeared in a number of films and television shows and authored three books. His comedy albums include 1959's *Inside Shelley Berman*, which was the first non-musical recording to win a Grammy Award. In recent years, Berman has acted in *Curb Your Enthusiasm* and *You Don't Mess with the Zohan*. He is lecturer emeritus at USC's Master of Professional Writing program.

Lowbrow designer MATTHEW BERUBE is a librarian living in Amherst, Massachusetts.

CARL CASSEL is an illustrator and graphic designer from Stockholm.

Portland, Oregon's CARSON ELLIS has provided art for books such as *The Mysterious Benedict Society*, by Trenton Lee Stewart, and *The Composer Is Dead*, by Lemony Snicket. She is illustrator-in-residence for the band the Decemberists.

NATHAN GELGUD is an artist who lives and works in Brooklyn. He has contributed illustrations to the *Believer* and comics to *Smoke Signal*, and often draws things for people on commission.

The New York painter JACKIE GENDEL has exhibited nationally and internationally. Her work has something to do with broken narrative arcs and her recent exhibition history is dotted with intriguing titles such as *Fables in Slang*, at Bryan Miller in Houston, *Rose Madder and the Ultramarines*, at Jeff Bailey in New York, and *Precarity and the Butter Tower*, at CTRL in Houston.

BEN GOLDBERG runs the record label Ba Da Bing and manages bands. He spent the '90s editing the overly ambitious zine *Badaboom Gramophone*. Recently, he has performed standup comedy to crowds whose stunned responses could not be chalked up as laughter.

FRANCESCA GRANATA holds a Ph.D. from Central Saint Martins University of the Arts London. She is an assistant professor at Parsons The New School for Design and editor of *Fashion Projects*, a journal on fashion, art and visual culture. She lives in Chelsea.

Lowbrow contributing editor NEIL MICHAEL HAGERTY has been responsible for varying aspects of the rock and roll bands the Howling Hex, Royal Trux and Pussy Galore. He is the author of the novel *Victory Chimp*, the essay collection *Public Works* and the comic book *The Adventures of Royal Trux*. An audiobook edition of *Victory Chimp* came out last year on Drag City.

The musician and record producer LEE HAZLEWOOD (1929–2007) was most famous for his work with Nancy Sinatra, including the hit "These Boots Are Made for Walkin'" and the 1968 album *Nancy & Lee*. His songs have been recorded by Elvis Presley, Frank Sinatra, Beck and other artists. *The Pope's Daughter*, Hazlewood's surreal account of working with the Sinatras, was published in 2002.

Writer and cartoonist SAM HENDERSON has published in *Nickelodeon*, DC Comics, several other places (including pornography) and back again. For a long time he did *The Magic Whistle*, which was a series but now exists as a one-panel gag strip. In 2001, he was a writer for *SpongeBob Squarepants*. *Scene But Not Heard*, a collection of *Nickelodeon* strips, was recently published by Top Shelf.

Little Rock's JAY JENNINGS has published humor in the *New York Times*, the *Los Angeles Times* and the anthology *Mirth of a Nation*. He also edited the book *Tennis and the Meaning of Life: A Literary Anthology of the Game* and is the author of *Carry the Rock: Race, Football, and the Soul of an American City*. He is a regular contributor to the *New York Times Book Review*.

The artist DOREEN KIRCHNER illustrated *The Adventures of Royal Trux* comic book as well as the cover art of various CDs. She makes up half of the band Sudden Ensemble and lives in the wilds of New Jersey.

M. SWEENEY LAWLESS is a writer/performer and dramaturg whose work appears in the books *101 Damnations, May Contain Nuts, More Mirth of a Nation, Any Body's Guess* and *Life's a Stitch: The Best of Contemporary Women's Humor*, as well as *McSweeneys Internet Tendency*. She lives in New York City.

JOHN MATHIAS is an artist who lives on the Jersey Shore. He has done work for the *Washington Post*, Simon & Schuster, Donna Karan, Matador Records and others. He drew all eight covers of the *Lowbrow Reader*, as well as that of this book.

MICHAELANGELO MATOS is the author of *Sign o' the Times*, the 33 1/3 book series's Prince entry, and is currently working on a history of American rave. He lives in Brooklyn.

The illustrations of ALEX EBEN MEYER have appeared in the *New York Times*, the *Wall Street Journal*, *Time*, *Slate* and other publications. He works out of the Pencil Factory.

PHILLIP NIEMEYER is a designer associated with Double Triple of Brooklyn.

Los Angeleno JOE O'BRIEN is a screenwriter and editor of the comedy zine *Flop Sweat*. His work has appeared in *Arthur*, *Dazed and Confused* and *McSweeneys Internet Tendency*.

MARGEAUX RAWSON (né Watson) has worked as an editor at *Vibe*, *Suede* and *Time Out New York*, a staff writer at *Entertainment Weekly*, and senior vice president of media relations at Universal Motown Records. Her work has appeared in *Rolling Stone*, *Interview*, *GQ*, *Marie Claire* and *O, The Oprah Magazine*.

MIKE REDDY is a graphic artist based in Brooklyn. His drawings have appeared in the *Believer*, the *Ganzfeld* and many packages for the Fiery Furnaces. He also designed the cover for the recent edition of Gilbert Rogin's *What Happens Next? + Preparations for the Ascent*.

GILBERT ROGIN was born in New York in 1929. Throughout the 1960s and '70s, he was a prolific contributor of fiction to the *New Yorker*. As a journalist, Rogin worked for 30 years at *Sports Illustrated*, ultimately as managing editor; he was later corporate editor of Time Inc. His two novels, *What Happens Next?* and *Preparations for the Ascent*, were issued as a single-volume edition in 2010 by Verse Chorus Press.

Editor JAY RUTTENBERG began publishing the *Lowbrow Reader* in 2001. He has written for the *New York Times*, *Puncture*, *Spin*, *Details* and *Time Out New York*, where he worked for many years as a music critic. He lives in Manhattan.

Lowbrow matriarch MARSHA ARONSON RUTTENBERG is a graduate of the University of Illinois and Northwestern University, and a lifelong Chicagoan.

TOM SANFORD is an artist who lives and works in Harlem. He has exhibited his paintings, drawings and in rare cases photographs all over the world.

DAN SULMAN is a standup comedian living in Boston.

JEFF WARD has written comedy for NBC, NPR and BBC Four. His essays have appeared in several anthologies of humorous prose. He is a member of ASCAP, the UAW and the BMI Workshop.

Boston journalist LIZA WEISSTUCH specializes in the spirits industry and cocktail and bar culture. She has contributed to the *New York Times*, the *Christian Science Monitor* and the *Boston Globe*, and is an American correspondent for *Whisky Magazine*.